Active Citizenship and Community Learning

Active Citizenship and Community Learning

To order, please contact our distributor: BEBC Distribution, Albion Close, Parkstone, Poole, BH12 3LL. Telephone: 0845 230 9000, email: learningmatters@bebc.co.uk. You can also find more information on each of these titles and our other learning resources at www.learningmatters.co.uk.

Active Citizenship and Community Learning

CAROL PACKHAM

Series Editors: Janet Batsleer and Keith Popple

LearningMatters

First published in 2008 by Learning Matters Ltd

British Library Cataloguing in Publication Data
A CIP record for this book is available from the British Library.

ISBN: 978 1 844 45152 4

Cover and text design by Code 5 Design Associates Ltd
Project Management by Swales & Willis Ltd
Typeset by Swales & Willis Ltd, Exeter, Devon
Printed and bound in Great Britain by TJ International Ltd, Padstow, Cornwall

Learning Matters Ltd
33 Southernhay East
Exeter EX1 1 NX
Tel: 01392 215560
info@learningmatters.co.uk
www.learningmatters.co.uk

FSC
Mixed Sources
Product group from well-managed
forests and other controlled sources
Cert no. SGS-COC-2482
www.fsc.org
© 1996 Forest Stewardship Council

Contents

Acknowledgements   vii

1 The context of active citizenship and
community learning   1

2 The role of the Youth and Community
Worker as informal educator   12

3 Civil and civic involvement and
'active citizens'   25

4 Volunteers and active citizens   42

5 The role of the Youth and Community
Worker in relation to volunteers   56

6 Enabling participation in communities   69

7 Inclusive and representative practice   86

8 Community based learning: learning by doing   105

9   **The effective practitioner**

119

10   **Taking the work forward**

138

Glossary   149

Index   152

Acknowledgements

I would like to acknowledge the contribution made to this book by the participants of the Take Part, Active Learning for Active Citizenship programme, especially those involved in the Greater Manchester hub: in particular, Anne Stewart, Carolina Oteyza, Kimberley Osivwemu, Shahida Sadiqu, Tanja Loncar, and Zoraida Mendiwelso-Bendek who gave me feedback on particular chapters or contributed case studies. Also the students on the Manchester Metropolitan University Youth and Community Work programmes who have already participated in many of the exercises used in the book. I would also like to recognize the contribution made to my thinking by being part of a group of volunteers and community activists in Whalley Range, Manchester, where, ironically, our campaigns and activities have had my reduced involvement during the writing of this book. I would also like to thank Tim for reading this, and for sharing our thinking as educators and partners.

The enthusiasm, insight and commitment of all the above to ongoing education and community activity continue to inspire me. Thank you.

Acknowledgements

Chapter 1

The context of active citizenship and community learning

This book is written as a contribution to the ongoing reflections of Youth and Community Workers regarding their relationship to the state and those with whom they work. The dilemmas evident in the book show the tensions between communities, who on the one hand are being called on to participate and have a voice in government processes from neighbourhood level up, whilst on the other are expected to voluntarily become part of processes of control, surveillance and welfare, often within communities that are already disadvantaged and excluded.

I make the case that Youth and Community Workers have an important role to enable community members to reflect on their experience in spaces for critical dialogue, which can bring about self directed change. I argue that critical, informal education based on Freirian approaches can be carried out with all types of volunteers, from those involved for primarily individual benefit to community activists, and that this is an important function of community learning.

This book draws on my experience as a Youth and Community Worker, volunteer and community activist in Manchester, and course leader of the BA in Youth and Community Work at Manchester Metropolitan University. It was brought together as the result of my involvement with the Home Office pilot Active Learning for Active Citizenship programme that ran from 2004 to 2006, and which contributed to the primary research for my Doctor of Education thesis. This book is therefore illustrated with a range of examples from these areas of ongoing practice.

The book provides exercises to help you think about the key themes of each chapter. They can be carried out individually or as part of a group, in line with the process of informal education. Many ask you to reflect on your own experience. The initial chapters give the social policy and theoretical context of our work, leading to specific chapters on work with different types of volunteers and carrying out community learning. The final chapters on enabling participation, inclusive, representative and reflective practice, although generally relevant raise particular issues in relation to citizenship and action.

The social policy context

Why this book, now? People have been involved in all types of voluntary activity throughout human existence; all involvement was voluntary before the establishment of paid employment. By the industrial revolution, those involved on a voluntary basis in Britain and her colonies were predominantly engaged in philanthropic activity to moralize, save or control those that they deemed to be a risk or at risk. Others were involved in self help activities within their communities or work places, and would most probably have been regarded as political agitators and viewed as a threat.

Recent interest in voluntary community engagement had stemmed from a variety of themes:

- Voluntary work experience can increase the range of skills and knowledge of a volunteer and so contribute to their future employability.

- Engaging in a voluntary capacity within communities and neighbourhoods contributes to social and individual well being.

- Social well being contributes towards social cohesion and a reduction in crime, antisocial behaviour, terrorism and extremism.

- Engagement in voluntary activity as part of a group can be an empowering and transformational experience leading to change and improvement (e.g. as part of a pressure or campaign group).

- Voluntary activity, particularly at the neighbourhood level, can improve the delivery of services and impact of initiatives at a local level (e.g. through community wardens).

- Active involvement can increase civic and civil engagement, and improve levels of involvement in governance, e.g. 'Citizens are now politically active in new ways and the challenge is to connect their activity to formal politics' (Goldsmith, 2008, p.3).

- Engagement of citizens (e.g. service users) in policy making can enable more effective and efficient delivery of services.

- Enforced community involvement can repay or contribute to society and 'do good', for example work undertaken by students, refugees and asylum seekers, and those serving community sentences for non-serious criminal offences.

- Volunteering is viewed as representing a step towards the achievement of full citizenship.

Voluntary involvement can therefore be seen to have moved beyond merely 'doing good' to being viewed as a means of developing good governance and community cohesion, as well as enhancing individual employability.

Garratt and Piper (2008), when discussing the development of volunteering initiatives, state that:

> *Since 1997, volunteering as a principle and practice has been promoted in a range of related areas of policy . . . volunteering may indeed extend the social and occupational experience and range of young people. It may also generate personal satisfaction, from helping others and acquiring self-knowledge. Through government funded schemes to encourage and channel voluntary activity, voluntary organizations of all sizes and types*

may achieve their social, educational or environmental aims. For all that, particular characteristics of this enthusiasm for volunteering suggest that the success of these initiatives may be limited, and may have unintended (and often unhelpful) consequences . . . voluntary work must be voluntary, and the current enthusiasm for ensuring that it occurs, obscures the fact that it is something that people cannot be made or paid to do. Being told that voluntary work is good for you or for the community will not ensure participation unless there is the prior capacity, drive, or motivation to become involved. (Garratt and Piper, 2008, p.56)

Piper indicates not all volunteering schemes are voluntary, and as a result may be counter-productive. Additionally, not all individuals are equally able to participate. Social exclusion and the distribution of power affect the ability to become involved citizens, and so stifle the ability of some to reach their own and their community's potential. The government is attempting to redress this through the Communities in Control White Paper (DCLG, 2008) and a range of other measures to enforce 'the duty' to involve citizens in decision making.

Alongside this has been an increased emphasis on citizenship, and voluntary and active citizenship as being a reflection of an individual's duty and obligations to the state. Recent government initiatives have therefore been influenced by a commitment to:

- better enable local people to hold service providers to account;

- place a duty on public bodies to involve local people in major decisions;

- assess the merits of giving local communities the ability to apply for devolved or delegated budgets. (Governance of Britain, 2007, pp.7–8)

Voluntary involvement and citizenship

The British government approach defines citizenship as a state that has to be acquired or granted, based on your commitment to the norms of society. This is evident in the Goldsmith Citizenship Review, which talks of 'the duty of allegiance owed by citizens to the UK . . . citizenship should be seen as the package of rights and responsibilities which demonstrate the tie between a person and a country (2008, p.1). This approach is different from that of citizenship being a status which is conferred on all people who live within that society and assumed as a right from birth.

The Citizenship Review identifies what the government can do to 'enhance the bond of citizenship' that we feel as shared citizens. The measures outlined in the review are aimed to 'promote a shared sense of belonging and may encourage citizens to participate more in society' (Goldsmith, 2008, p.7). These measures include: school citizenship manifestos and portfolios detailing work carried out with the community; reduced university tuition fees for young people who volunteer; citizenship ceremonies for young people and new citizens; and deliberation days to encourage debate before elections (Goldsmith, 2008, p.7).

From the above discussion it can be seen that there is increasing government attention being paid to what has historically been a private, individual matter of how you spend your 'free' time. The successful involvement of individuals within their communities and local decision making processes are now viewed as essential elements for cohesive communities and effective service delivery. It is therefore important that Youth and Community Workers consider how we relate to these government agendas, and consider the implications for the application of our principles and practice.

Citizenship and action

Enabling people to be active and take action within their communities has been the focus of community workers since the growth of community development in the 1960s in Britain. The first government-led initiatives in community capacity building were through the local authority based Community Development Projects, which proved too radical and challenging to the institutions that were funding them, and the projects were quickly disbanded. During the 1980s the Conservative government's approach denied the importance of community as 'political developments were centred on individuals and families pursing their own interests in the context of the market' (Woodd, 2007, p.8).

With the arrival of the New Labour government in 1997, social policy became influenced by views that the community was important both for the well being and solidarity of its members and for society as a whole. Based on the theories of communitarianism and the development of social capital, the then Home Secretary David Blunkett emphasized the concept of **active citizenship** and the 'idea that the freedom of citizens can only be truly realized if they are enabled to participate constructively in the decisions which shape their lives' (Woodd, 2007, p.8).

ACTIVITY 1.1

Think about the ways that you choose to help or benefit other people that you are not paid to undertake; divide these into:

- *activities that you may do on your own as an individual;*

- *activities that you carry out as part of a group;*

- *those that are part of informal arrangements;*

- *those that are part of formal structures.*

These categories can be used as the basis for identifying different types of **active citizen** involvement and are shown in the figure below. They will be discussed in Chapter 4.

From 1997 a raft of policy documents and initiatives were developed working towards civil renewal, including the introduction of the citizenship curriculum. David Blunkett identified the key government themes as being 'a shared belief in the power of education to enrich the minds of citizens, a commitment to develop a mutually supportive relationship amongst the members of a democratic community and a determination to strengthen citizens' role in shaping the public realm' (Home Office, 2003, p.3). He further identified the government role in trying to achieve these by stating 'instead of standing back and letting go of the values of solidarity, mutuality and democratic self determination, government – both central and local – has a vital role to play in strengthening community life and renewing civic involvement (Home Office, 2003, p.4). In the Home Office pamphlet *Active Citizens, Strong Communities – Progressing Civil Renewal* (2003) he made the case that this was an essential task for the development of strong communities and a way of avoiding a fragmented society.

Active citizens have therefore become a central element of government attempts to build community cohesion, devolve power to a community level, engage people in democratic processes, and help identify and meet local needs. Individuals may be active in a number of ways, as you would have identified through the above task. On an individual level this may be involvement in political processes through voting and by helping as a volunteer. Individuals can also participate through existing, formed structures, such as serving as school governors or on management committees of voluntary organizations. They may also participate in natural groups, such as campaigning groups at a local, national and global level, 'actively challenging unequal relations of power, promoting social solidarity and social justice, both locally and beyond, taking account of the global context' (Take Part, 2006, p.13).

The figure below shows different types of citizenship involvement, illustrating the connections between individual and collective actions and formal and formal engagement (based on NCVO, 2005).

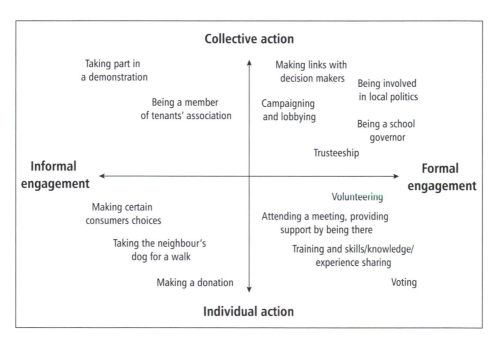

Figure 1.1 Citizen involvement (From www.takepart.org. p.13)

It is necessary for Youth and Community Workers to consider the different types of involvement, ranging from volunteers to active citizens and community activists, and our role in supporting and enabling this activity, and the learning processes this necessitates. The implications for Youth and Community Workers are discussed throughout this book.

Active Learning for Active Citizenship (ALAC)

The increased recognition of citizen activities and the involvement of community members at a community and group level has resulted in attention being paid to how they are trained and supported. Chapter 7 discusses the national curriculum for adult active citizens that was drawn up by David Blunkett as part of the ALAC pilot.

The ALAC pilot programme took place in seven areas across Britain, involving over a thousand people and drawing on existing activities being carried out by groups, enabling them to be involved in decision making at a local and sometimes national level.

> *One of the central features of ALAC has been the numerous ways in which participants have become more involved in civic life. This has encompassed becoming involved in volunteering for the first time and becoming more involved in volunteering with an emphasis on citizenship, becoming activists, getting involved in community groups and systems of governance and influencing service delivery. One of the overarching themes has been the ways in which participants have become engaged as individuals, and in addition have become more organized, knowledgeable and effective as members of groups and organizations when engaged in community activities. (Annette and Mayo, 2008, p.6)*

Involvement in activities is seen as having the potential for learning through experience. Education is also viewed as being necessary for effective involvement. The ALAC programme worked on the premise that learning is not essential for community action and activity, but that there is a role for informal learning to enable people to be more effective in the activities that they choose to undertake, as well as to help participants be more aware and better able to make informed decisions about their action and involvement.

As stated by the evaluators of the ALAC programme:

> *ALAC was based upon a community development approach. The emphasis was upon working democratically and learning collectively, through organizations and groups in the community. ALAC focused upon community empowerment through learning, enabling organizations and groups to enhance the effectiveness of their strategies for social change. Through increasing their knowledge and their critical understandings of power structures and decision-making processes, ALAC participants would be empowered to intervene and, where necessary, work towards changing these, in the pursuit of the values of equality and social justice. (Mayo and Rooke, 2006, p.16)*

A definition of **active citizenship** was drawn up by the programme:

> *Active citizenship is concerned with more than learning 'the rules of the game' and how to participate within existing models and structures . . . active citizenship should be defined more broadly to encompass active learning for political literacy and empowerment, addressing structures and relations of power and working to change these, where necessary, in the pursuit of social inclusion and social justice agendas (Lister, 1997). It also relates to how people can promote community cohesion and social solidarity, thereby strengthening civil society as well as empowering individual citizens. (Take Part, 2006, p.12)*

The programme therefore aimed to take a social justice approach to citizenship. Although at its inception it was supported by the Home Office, the direction of the work was strongly influenced by a Youth and Community Work, informal and popular education perspective. The ALAC participants rejected the proposed national curriculum for active citizenship and developed a learning framework (www.takepart.org) which 'would provide greater social inclusion and opportunities for accreditation and personal development . . . to counter the possibility of learning from negative experiences that might result in "political alienation and not active citizenship"' (Annette and Creasy, 2007, p.7).

Community learning

The community learning emphasis in this book is designed

- to distinguish between learning that takes place in formal settings that are not owned or controlled by the community;

- to indicate that there is a role for Youth and Community Workers in the community learning process;

- to establish that community based learning should meet certain criteria; ideally it should be based on community identified needs or interests and be of benefit to the community;

- to suggest that both Youth and Community Workers should be engaged in informal education.

Community learning is therefore not the same as community education, which tends to be formal education based in community settings, sometimes based on community needs and interests but most often being determined by the commissioner/funder, etc.

Both active citizenship and community based learning imply that participants are part of communities and neighbourhoods/localities to which they contribute and from which they gain. As discussed in the chapter on civic and civil engagement, the importance of community as having the potential for individual and group empowerment, particularly through the process of developing community cohesion, has been a growing theme of New Labour social policy in the UK. This book accepts the position that communities are not purely geographical and those individuals may belong to a number of communities, at personal, local and global levels, and be involved in a variety of different social arrangements.

Communities are always in flux. New ones are created and existing ones change, not only as a result of changing membership but also as a result of the impact of external forces. Crow and Maclean debate how people may choose to become part of a community that provides 'anchor points for an individuals' identity in an uncertain word' (2006, p.320). They also discuss how the impact of the global economy can challenge existing work, consumer patterns, and the composition of communities, and how the international media challenge and change internal community collective values. They state:

> the appeal to community is a powerful rhetorical device by which groups can seek to reinforce their solidarity, although . . . this is often achievable only by the exclusion of others. It follows that the more 'community' is interpreted differently according to

people's social class, gender, ethnicity, sexuality, age and health status, the greater the potential is to the focus of social conflicts. (Crow and Maclean, 2006, p.323)

Youth and Community Workers must acknowledge the importance of community as a space for collective learning, action and change. However, as stated above, communities are not homogenous. Their strength and potential lie within their diversity. A recognition of difference must not result in an exacerbation of the type of bonding capital that Putnam (2000) refers to, which solidifies groups and excludes 'outsiders'. Neither must it result in the targeting of some communities as being different and 'hard to reach', thereby encouraging programmes aimed at assimilation.

As Piper states:

behind the official rhetoric of local citizen participation and community partnership is frequently a concern to impose centrally determined and authoritarian structures on problematic neighbourhoods . . . there are clear grounds for doubt that the simplistic and positive approach to volunteering which characterizes government initiatives in citizenship education and elsewhere is likely to promote social justice. (Garratt and Piper, 2008, p.63)

Action and informal education

The theme of this book is action and how individuals feel empowered and confident to value and take their own actions. The chapters outline different elements of the process of action and how Youth and Community Workers can be involved in supporting the process of learning from action, particularly in relation to citizenship and other community activities. The role of the worker in the process of informal education through working in groups is outlined, with examples from practice. The theme 'action' indicates that the process of learning is not passive. This implies that participants can draw on and develop their own experience and practice and can

collectively develop strategies . . . through learning with other people, through practice rather than by absorbing theory . . . with conversation and dialogue as key tools to facilitate learning . . . by enabling people to gain new skills, insights and understanding through tackling real-life challenges in the community. (Take Part, 2006, p.8)

The name of the ALAC national programme was chosen to emphasize the importance of action and the learning by doing process.

People therefore draw on their own experience and previous actions; they use ongoing action as a basis for learning and development, and plan and take future action to bring about change. Active learning for active citizenship can therefore be seen to include being an active citizen, engaged in a range of endeavours, and learning from that action. This is not only a process of learning from experience but is also an ongoing process of reflection on that action and making decisions about future change and transformation. Crucially this process of critical dialogue is encouraged and supported by engagement with a critical community/group and facilitated in many cases by a skilled enabler, in our case a professional Youth and Community Worker.

Chapter 2 on informal education identifies the requirements for this process: the making of space for deliberation and reflection on action and experience; enabling participants to have control over what action is undertaken and how, and being proactive to ensure that all have the opportunity to participate by being inclusive and challenging oppressive structures and processes.

Chapter 3 discusses government policy in relation to civic and civil engagement, and what benefits are obtained through the undertaking of action. Robert Putnam's (2000) identification of different types of capital, social, human and physical, are discussed and a new element of state capital added to identify action that predominantly benefits the state/government and or civic processes.

Chapter 4 discusses differing types of volunteering and uses a volunteer type framework to identify the types of activity taking place, particularly in relation to the types of capital generated. The role of the worker in relation to different types of volunteers is then discussed in Chapter 5.

Chapter 6 discusses how the worker can enable the taking of action and participation, whilst Chapter 7 identifies the importance of inclusive and representative practice and the importance of being proactive at individual, cultural and structural levels.

Chapter 8 draws on the earlier chapters to identify how to enable learning environments and uses a framework showing the action learning process from inception to evaluation, and identifies the need to be clearer about what is achieved and for whom.

Chapter 9 discusses the elements of being an effective practitioner, drawing on reflection and levels of accountability. Dilemmas are raised and the possible strategy options identified.

Chapter 10 suggests the requirements for taking our work forward, including working with 'difference', making space, locating our practice and companion building.

The book aims to enable practitioners to be more effective critical practitioners, to locate their work in relation to social policy agendas and requirements, and show how they can work with active citizens through empowering and transformative informal education processes. This is an exercise in critical community practice (Butcher et al., 2007) and uses the processes of popular education as identified by Freire (1972), 'using dialogical methods of action learning' (Butcher et al., 2007, p.53). This is characterized by being learner centred, problem posing, bringing about concretization through praxis and critical dialogue, reflection, and a commitment to change and transformation. All are set in the context of a 'commitment to social justice' (ibid.).

Conclusion

This chapter has set the context for the themes that are explored in the following chapters in relation to the development of active citizenship and community learning. Issues have been raised regarding the development of government initiatives in areas that have been traditionally the focus for voluntary community involvement. The text aims to provide workers with theoretical frameworks and models for thinking about our practice in relation to these changes, whilst being anchored in an imperative that we have a role with individuals and groups as informal educators.

How to use this book

This book is written as a text for Youth and Community Work students and practitioners by an academic who is also a Youth and Community Work practitioner!

The book is designed for use as a full module, assuming an existing initial understanding of Youth and Community Work theory, knowledge of the historical development of the profession, the social division's concepts and practices, government and politics. The chapters build on each other, providing the elements to contribute towards the completion of a framework for facilitating effective community learning.

Each chapter includes case studies to illustrate the learning points and theory, and tasks to enable you to compile a portfolio of reflective activities which can contribute towards assessment. Many of these draw on experience and practice. References are given at the end of each chapter so that the chapters can be used independently.

The book draws on the work of the Active Learning for Active Citizenship pilots and makes reference to the Take Part learning framework which can be accessed at www.takepart.org/framework-for-active-learning.

As a whole, the book meets many of the Common Standards for Community Learning and Development, and the Professional and National Occupational Standards for Youth Work (see www.lifelonglearninguk.org for a full list of the standards).

Many of the most used terms are defined in the Glossary section.

REFERENCES

Annette, J and Creasy, S (2007) *Individual pathways to participation*. Swindon: ESRC.

Annette, J and Mayo, M (2008) eds., *Active learning for active citizenship.* Nottingham: NIACE.

Butcher, H, Banks, S, Henderson, P, and Robertson, J eds (2007) *Critical community practice*. Bristol: Policy Press.

Crow, G and Maclean, C (2006) Community, in G. Payne, ed. *Social divisions*. Basingstoke: Palgrave Macmillan, pp.305–324.

Department of Communities and Local Government (DCLG) (2008) *Communities in Control* White Paper. London: DCLG.

Freire, P (1972) *Pedagogy of the oppressed.* London: Penguin Books.

Garratt, D and Piper, H (2008) Volunteering and communitarian education policy, in *Citizenship education, identity and nationhood*. London: Continuum.

Goldsmith, Lord QC (2008) *Citizenship review. Citizenship; our common bond.* London: Ministry of Justice.

Governance of Britain (2007) Ministry of Justice. London: TSO.

Home Office (Blunkett, D) (2003) *Active citizens, strong communities – progressing civil renewal*. London: Home Office.

Ledwith, M (1997) *Participating in transformation.* Birmingham: Venture Press.

Mayo, M and Rooke, A (2006) *Active learning for active citizenship: An evaluation report.* London: Goldsmiths College.

Putnam, RD (2000) *Bowling alone: The collapse and revival of American community.* New York: Simon and Schuster.

Take Part (2006) *The national framework for active learning for active citizenship.*

Woodd, C (2007) Active learning for active citizenship: The policy context. *OR Insight,* 20 (2): 8–12.

WEBSITES

Occupational standards at www.ukstandards.org

For full text of *Citizenship review* see www.justice.gov.uk

www.takepart.org

Chapter 2

The role of the Youth and Community Worker as informal educator

Introduction

In this chapter the importance of work with groups is emphasized. The three characteristics of informal education can be identified as

- making space for association and deliberation;
- enabling self directed involvement and action;
- using a critical perspective that enables inclusion and participation.

The term informal education and its practice is usually used in relation to work with young people. I make the case that the process and principles of informal education are essential for all the work that we as Youth and Community Workers undertake. An informal education approach is an essential element of our role to enable the process of community based education and active citizenship – what Smith and Jeffs call 'fostering democracy and association' (2007, np).

The principles central to Youth and Community Work practice is that the work is collective, participatory and inclusive, and involves people in an active educational process. The aims being to bring about social justice, critical awareness, transformation and change. The characteristics are that the work should be identified by the participants, preferably in a setting determined by them, and that they should have control over the process of the work. Informal education does not mean that the learning and education process is unstructured. How the work is carried out might be planned and structured, as in some of the active citizenship programmes, but the participants will be engaged in work within groups formed or natural, learning from their experience and practice.

Identifying these key elements of our work will help us to think critically about our practice and locate what we do in relation to other approaches and other professions. For example in Popple's (1995) models of community work practice, community education is one of several types of intervention:

- community care and community organization where the worker has more of an organizational role;

- community development and social planning where the worker acts as a self help enabler;

- community action and radical approaches, where the worker is a co-activist, or ally.

Likewise in Mark Smith's typology (1988) the youth worker as educator is only one of several approaches including that of provider of leisure and welfare worker.

Margaret Ledwith has critiqued models of community work in relation to how they lend themselves to a more critical understanding of practice. In relation to this *community care* 'which is preoccupied with the welfare of groups perceived as vulnerable in the community' (Ledwith, 1997, p.106), is not deemed to 'contribute to collective action for change'. Ledwith locates *community organization* as a traditional approach tending 'to focus on improving levels of welfare provision' (ibid., p.107) and may include adult education classes, but this approach is also viewed as 'not moving towards critical consciousness and they do nothing to combat poverty and inequality'. Both of these approaches have a reliance on the worker to initiate action.

Community development meets many of Ledwith's requirements for community empowerment, with the worker's role as one facilitating self identified change. However, she critiques the approach as too often failing to set action in a wider political context and assuming that problems can be solved by local action alone, for example, coordinated action and cooperation. *Community action*, however, is a self help activity, action being taken based on a critical structural analysis of local issues by local people. Ledwith critiques this approach for too often failing to take into account inequalities of power, for example the exclusion of women and black people. Both community development and community action require the worker to work with community participants to facilitate change. Ledwith argues for a *Core Values Model* of community intervention, the elements of which are similar to the characteristics of informal education that are set out in this chapter.

The characteristics of informal education

What characterizes informal education is the commitment and practice of dialogical education based on the learner's high levels of active participation, with a distinctive role for the worker as facilitator and enabler.

In 1990 Jeffs and Smith stated that informal education was an emerging practice which crosses traditional demarcation lines. They argued for the recognition of it as being a type of education that could take place in a range of settings and that had particular characteristics. These characteristics have been summarized by Banks (1999) as being that

> the process is based on dialogue, it works with cultural forms that are familiar to participants, participation is voluntary, it takes place in a variety of settings, it has educational goals . . ., and makes use of experiential as well as assimilative patterns of learning. (1999, p.7)

These characteristics draw very heavily on the key elements of the 'popular education' process developed by Paulo Freire (1921–1997), the Brazilian educationalist, who has had a significant impact on Youth and Community Work approaches. Since the 1970s his philosophy and practice has been adopted as giving a framework for our work, particularly in relation to its informal education focus and critical/ideological perspective. As discussed in the *Pedagogy of the Oppressed* (1972) and repeatedly reflected upon in his later works, particularly *Pedagogy of Hope* (1992) and one of his last works, *Teachers as Cultural Workers, Letters to Those Who Dare Teach* (1998), Freire's main themes are dialogue, praxis, conscientization, using experience and problem posing.

Dialogue is a process of conversational encounter and exploration with others, including the worker, which enables critical analysis of the world. **Praxis** is the process of reflection and the taking of informed political action, drawing on theory and values such as respect for others, and a commitment to human well being (Freire, 1998). **Conscientization** is the name given by Freire to the process of becoming aware, 'learning to perceive social, political and economic contradictions and to take action against the oppressive elements of reality' (1972, p.15) regarding their situation of oppression by becoming literate, using experience, and using problem posing and enquiry, as opposed to what he called a banking method of teaching. As a **problem posing** education, this means that both worker and participant are engaged in a process of critically exploring reality, and so re-creating knowledge. In his view this meant that those involved were not 'pseudo-participants' but were undertaking 'committed involvement' (Freire, 1972, p.44). The role of the worker was therefore as a partner and facilitator of the educational process.

Through these methods he hoped that a process of transformation and change would take place, that people's new knowledge and insights would lead them to change the structures, situations and institutions that had been oppressing them (Mayo, 1997).

Importantly, he saw that education was not a neutral process.

> *Education either functions as an instrument which is used to facilitate the integration of (people) into the logic of the present system and bring about conformity to it, or it becomes the 'practice of freedom', the means by which men and women deal critically and creatively with reality and discover how to participate in the transformation of their world. (Shaull, 1972. p.14)*

This practice of freedom ultimately leads those involved in the educational process to become independent and liberated from the educator.

Young charts the development of informal education and the influence of Freirian thinking stating that 'more recently the term 'informal education has emerged . . . to characterize a particular form of practice that has at its heart, the idea of 'critical dialogue or conversation' (1999, p.22).

The value of conversation, or critical dialogue, was also advocated by informal education theorists such as Jeffs and Smith (1999), in *Informal Education, Conversation, Democracy and Learning*, where they state that 'informal educators work in a multitude of ways. They exploit and create learning opportunities. Central to their work is the fostering of conversation, working so that people can engage with each other and the world' (1999, p.3).

The components of Freirian popular education will be illustrated in this chapter. Added to these are a set of core values, respect for basic human and individual rights, respect for difference, a commitment to empowerment and participatory democracy, collective action and voluntary (consenting) participation.

Work with groups enables informal education to take place, and so provides the potential for action and change. There are three main requirements for this process: *making space for association and critical dialogue, enabling self directed involvement and action, using a critical perspective that enables inclusion and participation.*

1. Making space for association and critical dialogue

One of the defining characteristics of informal educators is the ability and aim to facilitate the making of 'space', or what has been called the learning environment, for critical dialogue, which enables political agency and voice (Batsleer and Humphries, 2000). This space provides the opportunity for those with whom we work to discuss their experiences of the world and *their* world. This process of educational enquiry can be undertaken with groups or organizations, and at a participant, worker or interagency level.

Payne (2001) identified the benefits of working with and through groups:

- Participation in groups is a usual occurrence for people and one that most value.

- The demands of group life give the potential for growth.

- Groups can be supportive for isolated individuals but also in relation to sharing tasks and ideas.

- Groups can help bring about social change through consciousness raising.

- More can be achieved collectively than individually. (Payne, 2001)

The educational process of working with groups has been referred to as a 'social theory of learning'. Wenger (2006) identifies this as a process that enables the development of the individual ('learning as becoming'), draws on the communities within which they engage ('learning as belonging'), and learns from experience and practice.

Facilitated productive discussion, dialogue or what some have called deliberation is an essential element of this group process. It enables people to develop awareness and self confidence. As stated by Batsleer, 'the aim of consciousness raising conversation is to enable people to come to voice and to enable aspects of the self that may usually be silenced to emerge. It encourages people to name their own realities rather than simply adapt to the ways in which their realities are named for them' (Batsleer, 2008, p.29). The group process can also identify areas for action, as 'conversation may be conceived as a process of coming to voice, and then of using that voice to investigate and explore reality, in a collaborative rather than competitive way . . . themes emerge from the realities of the participants in conversation . . .' (ibid., p.19, p.14).

The relevance and importance of the concept of critical dialogue emerged through the national meetings for the Active Learning for Active Citizenship (ALAC) pilot. Discussions between the core pilot programmes recognized that although they were delivering very different types of activity, one of the shared methodologies was the commitment to enabling critical dialogue within groups. This was being carried out with a range of different groups focusing on differing themes, for example, developing the ability of women to speak out and engage in decision making structures in the West Midlands; community groups debating local issues and agreeing priorities for action in Manchester; and the establishment of 'constructive conversations' between migrant workers, employers and service providers in the agricultural areas of Lincolnshire.

The concept and requirement of space is important, the word becoming an acronym to encapsulate the key element of the ALAC work – Social Political and Active Citizenship Education (SPACE) (source, Ted Hartley, South Yorkshire Workers Education Association, ALAC, 2005). This is being used to signify the opportunities that are required to enable reflective educational practice for change.

A report from the National Council for Voluntary Organizations, 'Civil Renewal and Active Citizenship', also recognizes the importance of space:

> *for argument and deliberation, in which citizens can express their different viewpoints and negotiate a sense of the common interest, . . . Key here is civil society as a space in which citizens can debate what the 'good society' means – how social , economic and political progress can be defined. It is also as space in which people come together voluntarily, in other words the space in which voluntary association and voluntary action occur. (Jochum et al., 2005, pp.7–8)*

The Youth and Community Worker's role in the making and enabling of space for these interactions is therefore essential.

The importance of working with groups and the creation of space for deliberation is that the educator can provide a situation in which participants can 'stop, reflect critically on what they are doing, identify new information or skills they may need, get training and plan further action'(Stewart, 2008, NWCN workshop). The importance of enabling people to become more aware through discussing issues as part of groups is an essential prerequisite for taking action. As Batsleer states:

> *group work has long been valued as a democratic method, as contributing to the development of civil society, and to the critique of pathologizing discourses in social policy. It can create a basis for mutual support and self help in an increasingly individualized society, and is frequently cited as contributing to the development of social capital. (Batsleer, 2008, p.55)*

CASE STUDY

The work of the Black Country Hub working with women to explore their involvement in decision making through the Impact! programme illustrates this approach.

The Impact! approach to creating a safe space for learning starts with the individual and then shares it with a group. Impact! believes that there are four essential ingredients which combine to create the conditions for women (and other marginalized groups) to be confident and active in the public domain.

These four ingredients are:

- *valuing your own skills;*
- *knowing yourself through and with others;*
- *knowing how the external world operates; and*
- *knowing where to go to get what you need.*

This approach challenges the notions of individualism and competition by bringing women together in association, collectively to reflect upon and analyse the barriers to, and opportunities for creating change for themselves and others. Impact! suggests that once women make these connections and see their own concerns reflected in the struggles of others, they can collectively develop strategies around how to overcome the barriers and make positive changes.

In the Impact programmes the facilitators have worked in different ways to create safe spaces where we encourage a 'respectful discourse'; where we can get beyond assumptions around education, work, marriage, sex, tradition, faith, class, age, culture, housework, children, politics and power – where we can 'hear the hurt'. These are spaces for difficult discussions and joint celebrations, spaces to explore what shapes and shaped us and what we want to do about this. 'We were very clear that we wanted women to challenge the way that things are currently happening – to become 'awkward citizens' .Our approach to creating a safe space for learning requires that we always start with and from the experiences and knowledge of the individual learner, thereby involving the learner as a participant in the learning process. We then share this in the group context, creating a collective pool of knowledge and experiences.

The programme was a mix of workshops, residential events, field visits, events and support sessions running over a 6–9 month period, depending upon the nature of the group. In previous years we have held what is called 'round table' events, where women who are active in public and community life come to share their stories with other women. Following the Impact! learning programme participants have increased levels of confidence, skills and knowledge and are more politically aware:

> *I believe I can change things.*

Participants have learned more about themselves, their differences and collective experiences. They have surprised themselves, challenged the barriers of discrimination and have a better understanding of others:

> *Everyone boosted each other's confidence by telling their own experiences and listening to each other.*

They have recognized the needs of their own communities, organized their political lives, become involved in different issues and made global links:

> *I now help others to build their confidence and realize their potential. I am planning to set up a Women's Enterprise Development Agency.*

Participants feel – and are – more influential:

> *I have influence on how my kids are looked after in school. I feel confident that I can get people involved – to challenge and change structures.*

> *(Take Part (2006) The national framework for active learning for active citizenship. London: DCLG, p.71, www.takepart.org/framework-for-active-learning)*

To enable informal education to take place within these spaces it is also crucial that participants have control, agency and self determination over their space, both in relation to the content of the dialogue that takes place and to the participants' voluntary engagement.

2. Self directed, voluntary involvement and action

Voluntary involvement refers to the participant's free choice to undertake activities, and ideally their control over the choice of activities. This results in a high level of participation; the Youth and Community Worker's role in enabling participation is discussed in Chapter 6. Voluntary involvement also includes the ability of citizens to choose and undertake activities in a process of self help and community action.

However, while participants might be able to negotiate the content or focus of the work, it does not necessarily mean that they have a say in whether they participate. Youth and Community Workers are increasingly working in settings and with participants who have not chosen to take part, for example with young people attending Pupil Referral Units, or with young people in the Criminal Justice System or adults undertaking Community Service Orders. For many Youth and Community Workers the principle of voluntary engagement is one of the key characteristics of informal education. Ord (2007), however, argues that voluntary involvement is in itself not necessary or sufficient, and states:

> *ultimately it is the quality of the relationship which forms out of the engagement, the degree of choice at the disposal of the participants, and the participative practices of the workers, not simply whether the project was based on the participants being able to chose to attend that defines the potential of (youth work) practice. (Ord, 2008, np)*

The characteristic of self directed active engagement requires that the participants should undertake action based on self identified needs and issues, a process of problem posing, and that they identify what action needs to be taken The activity is not undertaken as problem solving, for example responding to someone else's perceived identification of local needs. Ord would argue that this can take place even if the participants have not volunteered to be involved in the work.

The distinction between problem posing as opposed to being expected to solve issues and problems (for example antisocial behaviour) has been important in the debates within the ALAC pilots and the role that the then Home Office, now the Department of Communities and Local Government, envisages for active citizens. Although having a commitment to community involvement, the 'government' approach is primarily one for assisting in solving problems such as 'developing our approach to build a safe, just and tolerant society . . . helping to build active, cohesive and empowered communities' (Home Office, 2005, p.3).

In contrast, the Freirian or popular education model that is adopted by Youth and Community Workers suggests that 'the whole of education and development is seen as a common search for solutions to problems. From the beginning all participants are recognized as thinking, creative people with the capacity for action. The aim of the educator is to help them identify the aspects of their lives which they want to change, to identify the problems' (Stewart, 2008, np). This is an educational process of problem posing by the group, followed by reflection and critical analysis of that problem through dialogue, with the view of leading to action and change.

The element of action or active engagement is a defining characteristic of informal education, as opposed to formal education which often takes a directed, didactic and non-experiential approach to education. The self directed nature of participation, as well as requiring that participants choose to take part, requires that participants should also have control over the content and outcomes of the activity and educational content (the curriculum) and process. This principle was central to the work of the ALAC pilot projects. The participating groups were initially asked to pilot a draft national curriculum for active citizenship laid down by the then Home Secretary (see Woodward, 2004).The pilot projects found the concept of a national curriculum for ALAC too restrictive and controlling, (reminiscent of the core Youth and Community Work curriculum debates of the 1980s), counter to the ethos of ALAC, and unable to meet the individual needs and interests of the diverse groups we are working with. The ALAC hubs therefore argued for and then drew up a 'learning framework' that can be locally interpreted and negotiated by the participants. This uses a popular education model.

ACTIVITY 2.1

Log onto the Take Part, active learning for active citizenship home page and access the learning framework (www.takepart.org/framework-for-active-learning).

This framework outlines many of the important features of ALAC that are discussed in this book. Sections 3.1 and 4 give examples of case studies from across the seven regions that make up the Take Part network.

---

3. Using a critical perspective, enabling inclusion and participation

The third characteristic of the informal educator is that of holding and applying an ideological or critical perspective (Guba, 1990). A critical perspective is used within research to identify an approach that, unlike empirical and scientific research, takes as its starting point an assumption that our interventions within society are not value free or neutral.

Butcher et al. (2007), in their book *Critical Community Practice*, discuss the different types of critical approach within community practice. Firstly, an approach is taken that criticizes something, that critiques or stands outside and inspects and evaluates.

Secondly, they invoke Brechin, 2000, in identifying a particular type of community practice which has three practitioner attributes:

- an open minded and reflective approach, e.g. taking into account the context
- working from a firm foundation of values and assumptions, e.g. social justice
- the ability to engage in a process of continual review and professional enquiry.

Their third use of the term 'critical practice' refers to 'practitioners developing and deploying a particular kind of "practice model" to guide and make sense of their work' (Butcher et al., 2007, p.10), the key components of which are initially having a 'critical conscious-ness', then undertaking 'critical theorizing', 'critical action' and 'critical reflection'. Again this model of practice draws on and is similar to the characteristics of popular education based on the Freirian approach (1972), and the process of reflective practice is discussed further in Chapter 9 on the reflective effective practitioner.

Using a critical perspective in relation to the three characteristics of informal education discussed here has elements of the types of critical practice discussed by Butcher et al. In this book I refer primarily to the commitment to social justice and inclusion which has as a key element a consideration of power relations and empowerment. As Ledwith states, 'If we are working towards consciousness and collective action for change with groups, within which issues of power and hierarchy are ignored, we are not likely to be successful' (Ledwith, 2005, p.162).

The critical perspective makes a structural analysis of causes of inequality and injustice, not one primarily based on the deficits of the individual. It therefore necessitates an approach where whole communities act in inclusive ways, which serve to bridge as opposed to bond and isolate others (Putnam, 2000). The role of the informal educator is key to enabling critical intelligence which will make a difference (Mayo and Thompson, 1995), both for workers and those with whom they work. Critical professionals therefore have a key role in enabling explorations of power and any subsequent change, similar to Freire's (1972) notion of dialogue, conscientization, praxis and transformation.

A critical perspective with a commitment to anti-discriminatory and inclusive practice necessitates reflective practice on behalf of the informal educator, and action to challenge discrimination and reduce exclusion. The worker's role is to enable the identification of areas of exclusion and oppression and facilitate action. As educators our role is therefore to enable self help for those with whom we work, ensure that we recognize difference and particular requirements, and that action is taken on a rights based approach (Crimmens and Wales, 1999). This means that we may work in alliance with individuals and groups where we do not share their experience but may share their perspective. We may challenge and engage in critical dialogue with those whose perspective we do not share.

In the case of the work of the ALAC pilot, although some specific groups of people and particular issues were identified, the nature of the work was holistic and self determined by many of the groups involved. For example, a School of Participation in Longsight, Manchester, worked together to develop greater local networking; a team of volunteers from a Healthy Living Network carried out an evaluation of the work of their team and the impact of their network on local groups.

Informal education in practice, the Hattersley Neighbourhood Partnership Audit

In 2006, the community development worker for the Hattersley Neighbourhood Partnership (Hattersley is a large, originally council owned overspill estate to the east of Manchester, built in the 1960s to house 9,000 people) identified, through conversations with representatives of local community groups, the need to evaluate the impact of the work of the partnership and to make suggestions for the future, after the work of the partnership had ended in 2007. A group of eight women, all volunteers with local groups and living within the area, volunteered to take part in what was to become an audit and evaluation of 31 local groups. They became a team which met on a regular monthly basis to decide how best to undertake the work, and with whom.

Although the work of the team was focused on the audit, the meetings became a space to discuss many related local and national issues, including the reputation of the estate, the role of volunteers, tenant management, national government policy and how to influence it, and how to organize and run events. The specific work of the audit focused on different research approaches, discussions of ethics, accountability, how to report back, the importance of participation and inclusion, and analysing data.

The role of the informal educator was to work with the community development worker and the group to facilitate the process of learning, and to support the team in undertaking the work. Space was created for the team to discuss and debate issues, and to make decisions. The participants volunteered to take part in a process which was based on their direct experience and needs, and which they hoped would benefit themselves and their community and groups. The informal educator was able to enable the team to draw on their local knowledge, networks and skills, so building their confidence and capacity to undertake work in the future.

A critical approach was apparent at a number of levels. Discussions about who should be involved and how enabled the team to identify people who might not be served by groups. As a result, a sample of 40 individuals who did not attend were interviewed. Issues of power and participation were discussed in relation to the work of the partnership, and in relation to government initiatives, such as tenant management in which several of the group were becoming involved nationally.

The team has been involved in ALAC work at a regional level by participating in hub events, and presenting their work at a workshop of the regional launch of the ALAC learning framework in November 2006. At a national level they have taken part in national ALAC events, and have built their confidence to participate in other consultation events held by the Department of Communities and Local Government, directly contributing to civic engagement and state capital. At a community and civil society level they have engendered social capital by influencing the future design of support and funding to local groups.

ACTIVITY **2.2**

Considering the examples in the Take Part learning framework, and the three characteristics of the informal education process outlined above, identify an issue or need that has been voiced by a group. Consider how you can make this into an informal education process enabling community learning to take place, using the requirements set out below. First state who the group is that you are working with, what issue or theme is to be the focus of the group's 'deliberations' and action, and the context of the work, e.g. history of the group/project, and factors affecting the work of the group.

Record how you will

- *make 'space' for dialogue and action, and for informal education to take place. How will you enable critical reflection to take place, discussing the focus at an individual, group and societal level?*

- *ensure that the process of the work has high levels of participation by the community and is self directed. How can the work bring about change and transformation?*

- *enable involvement and representation in the process of the activity. How does the work recognize and challenge inequalities of power and access?*

Informal education as a contribution to democracy

Jeffs and Smith (1999) in their work on 'Informal Education, conversation, democracy and learning' draw out the connection between informal education, association and democracy. In government documentation this is sometimes encapsulated into 'engagement'. They make the case that there are two reasons for this connection: firstly, that 'our focus on conversation expresses and fosters values, and ways of being with each other, that are central to democracy' (1999, p.25); secondly, that the organizations in which we work usually have democratic structures that provide a chance for learning and engaging in politics. Smith and Jeffs also suggest that informal educators should undertake 'democratic audits' (2007) of the work that they undertake to evaluate the contribution of their work to the fostering of democracy and association.

ACTIVITY **2.2** *continued*

Using the informal education activity you have outlined above carry out your own 'democratic audit' using the elements identified by Smith and Jeffs (2007) as set out below. Consider and record if the activity you have facilitated:

- *enabled all to share in a common life?*

ACTIVITY 2.2 continued

- *encouraged people to think critically?*
- *fostered the values and attitudes of a free society?*
- *sustained and extended opportunities for political participation?*
- *contributed towards greater equality?*

Conclusion

This chapter has identified the key characteristics of the informal education approach.

These are essential elements to complement and counter current government social policy initiatives such as the ALAC pilot. The role of the informal educator in creating space for self determined and inclusive work with groups will enable the continued development of vibrant, active and challenging citizens and communities. As Jeffs and Smith state in relation to the role of informal education in fostering democracy, 'these matters are not marginal to our task as educators – they are central. The cultivation of the knowledge skills and virtues necessary for political participation is more important morally than any other purpose of public education in a democracy' (Jeffs and Smith, 1999, p.33).

As shown in the examples above from the Impact programme and work with volunteers in Hattersley, informal education can make an important contribution to human, social and state capital, and what Mayo (1997) terms transformation. The potential and dilemmas raised from this work are discussed in the following chapter on civil and civic involvement.

REFERENCES

Annette, J and Creasy, S (2007) *Individual pathways to participation*. London: ESRC.

Batsleer, J and Humphries, B eds (2000) *Welfare, exclusion and political agency.* London: Routledge.

Banks, S ed. (1999) *Ethical issues in youth work*. London: Routledge.

Batsleer, J (2008) *Informal learning in youth work*. London: Sage.

Brechin, A ed. (2000) *Critical practice in health and social care.* London: Open University Press/Sage.

Butcher, H, Banks, S, Henderson, P, and Robertson, J (2007) *Critical community practice*. Bristol: Policy Press.

Crimmens, D and Whales, A (1999) A rights based approach to work with young people, in S Banks, ed. *Ethical issues in youth work.* London: Routledge.

Edwards, M (2005) *Civil society.* London: Polity Press.

Freire, P (1972) *Pedagogy of the oppressed.* London: Penguin Books.

Freire, P (1992) *Pedagogy of hope.* New York: Continuum.

Freire, P. (1998) *Teachers as cultural workers: Letters to those who dare teach.* Oxford: Westview Press.

Guba, E. (1990) *The alternative paradigm dialog*, in E Guba, ed. *The paradigm dialog*. London: Sage, pp.17–22.

Home Office (2005) *Communities group strategic plan 2005–6. Helping to build active, cohesive and empowered communities*. London: TSO, Home Office.

Jeffs, T and Smith, M eds (1990) *Using informal education*. Milton Keynes: Open University Press.

Jeffs, T and Smith, M (1999) *Informal education: Conversation, democracy, learning*. Tucknall: Education Now.

Jochum, V, Pratten, B and Wilding, K (2005) Civil renewal and active citizenship: A guide to the debate. A report from the National Council for Voluntary Organizations: London: NCVO.

Ledwith, M (1997) *Participating in transformation*. Birmingham: Venture Press.

Ledwith, M (2005) *Community development: A critical approach*. Bristol: BASW/Policy Press.

Mayo, M and Thompson, J eds. (1995) *Adult learning: Critical intelligence and social change*. Leicester: National Association of Adult Continuing Education.

Mayo, M (1997) *Imagining tomorrow. Adult education for transformation.* Leicester: NIACE.

Ord, J (2007) *Youth work process, product and practice*. Dorset: RHP.

Ord, J (2008) *Thinking the unthinkable, youth work without voluntary participation*. Youth and Policy Conference plenary paper. Leeds, March.

Payne, M (2001) Doing projects, in LD Richardson and M Wolfe, eds, *Principles and practice of informal education.* London: Routledge Falmer, pp.186–207.

Popple, K (1995*) Analysing community work*. Buckingham: Open University Press.

Putnam, RD (2000) *Bowling alone: The collapse and revival of American community.* New York: Simon and Schuster.

Shaull, R (1972) Foreword, in P Freire, *Pedagogy of the oppressed.* London: Penguin Books.

Smith, M (1988) *Developing youth work, informal education, mutual aid and popular practice.* Milton Keynes: Open University Press.

Smith, M and Jeffs, T (2007) Fostering democracy and association (www.infed.org).

Stewart, A (2008) Popular education workshop. Drawing on Partners, Training for Transformation, North West Citizenship Network Conference, Manchester Metropolitan University. Dublin: Partners.

Take Part (2006) The national framework for active learning citizenship. London: DCLG. See http://www.takepart.org.

Wenger, E (2006) A social theory of learning, in R Harrison and C Wise, eds, *Working with young people.* London: Open University Press/Sage, pp.142–149.

Woodward, V (2004) *Active learning for active citizenship*. London: Home Office, Civil Renewal Unit.

Young, K (1999) *The art of youth work.* Dorset: Russell House Publishing.

Chapter 3

Civil and civic involvement and 'active citizens'

As outlined in the introduction, the UK government's emphasis on recognizing and encouraging community involvement, at a group and individual level, has important implications for Youth and Community Workers. As an informal educator, the people with whom we work and the actions undertaken can never be seen in isolation. Some activities will be predominantly for the benefit of the community member and their community, whilst others may be primarily to support government initiated polices and structures, or the determination and delivery of services.

There is a worldwide trend to include the community in civic engagement. This chapter discusses different types of government initiatives in relation to communities and their members, and aims to raise levels of awareness about whose purpose it serves and most importantly 'for whose benefit'. This critique is not to undervalue the important opportunities afforded by the government's recognition of the value of the community and voluntary sector and volunteers, but to enable us as workers and those involved in voluntary activity to make informed decisions about how we spend our limited time and resources. The difference between local authority and government initiatives to increase community involvement in governance and the delivery of services (civic action) as opposed to citizens own initiatives (civil action) as evidenced in community action and self help is discussed and examples given.

ACTIVITY 3.1

List at least four groups or organizations that you are involved with in an unpaid capacity. If you are not involved, ask someone that you know, a neighbour, friend or relative, who is. This could be with a school, community group, sports club, etc. Complete the table below, naming the group or organization. Consider how they were formed, who by and what for. Whose interests and purpose do they serve and why?

Name of group Example: Sure Start centre	How it was formed Example: council said had we to have one	Who set the group up Example: council	Why the group was set up? Example: government policy	Whose interest/ purpose does it serve and why? Example: local authority, government
Example: Mothers Against Violence	Local publicity	Local mothers	To stop our children getting killed	Communities, young people and government. Reducing gang, gun and knife crime

You can see from the activity table above that there are very different types of groups and organizations, established for different purposes.

'Whose benefit? Locating our practice, thinking critically about 'whose purpose and interest' activity serves

From your own experience it should be evident that some activities are established from the community as a result of self identified needs and interests, whereas others may have come about as a result of government funding or local authority (LA) initiatives, externally identified priorities or perceived community needs.

As a further example, the table below illustrates a community activist's involvement in a number of inner city groups. This same table is discussed in Chapter 6. In relation to the types of participation involved.

The Labour government has placed a great emphasis on community engagement, involving community members in having a say about services and, in some cases, in how they are delivered, a task that in the past was carried out by the local authority. (For example the Friends of Manley Park listed in the table below, where the group undertakes bulb planting and litter picking.)

Table 3.1 Analysing group involvement

Name of group	How it was formed	Who set up the group	Why was the group set up?	Whose purpose does it serve and why?
Ward coordination	Council ward coordinator recruited officers, local group representatives, councillors	Council	Government policy	Councils, governments, community? Improve effectiveness of delivery of services, save money?
Police, local area partnerships/ neighbourhood policing	Police inspector called meeting of relevant people	Police	Government policy	Police, government, maybe community? Improve effectiveness of delivery of services, save money?
Community network	Local groups asked for representatives on the basis of themes and geographical areas	Local Strategic Partnership, asked for lead bodies from community groups	Government policy	City, government, community groups, communities
Strategic regeneration framework	Council decided areas and themes	Council	Government policy and city attempt at holistic look at areas and needs	City, local authority, community? Improve effectiveness of delivery of services, save money?
W/R forum	Local idea – public meeting, local publicity and local meetings	Representatives of local groups and community members	Locally identified need for a voice and to take action on local issues	Community, local groups, council?
Celebrate community festival	Local idea, and some available space and talent	Residents and representatives of groups	To have fun, bring the community together and show local talent	Community, local groups, service providers, government
Friends of Manley Park	Public meeting and local publicity	Council officers and community/users	To improve facilities in the park. LA and government initiative	Local authority, community, government Improve effectiveness of delivery of services, save money?
Friends of Al Buraq	Word of mouth in local networks	Local women (mainly Pakistani), some input from local groups e.g. Celebrate	To provide activities for local women and children who don't access services	Community, LA and government?

A result of the increase in statutory groups requiring community representation is that community members are expected to be involved in more and more meetings, most of the time without pay. Further, this may distract them from carrying out self help activities in the community.

This chapter aims to explore the implications of this involvement both for the community member and Youth and Community Worker.

Civil and civic involvement

ACTIVITY **3.2**

Make a list of all of the terms or expressions that you know that include the terms civic and civil. Based on what you think the terms civic and civil involvement mean draw up your own definition of the two terms.

From your list you will have started to see that the terms civic and civil are often used interchangeably, but that they are used to refer to different types of activity and organization, for example civil servants, the civic centre. However, it is important to understand the distinction between the two terms and the concepts they represent in order to locate our practice. We also need to understand the changes that are taking place in relation to government social policy, and its relationship to those involved in voluntary activity within these two spheres.

Popple (2000) states that **civil** society consists of 'organizations such as political parties, trade unions, churches and cultural, charitable and community groups . . . and is the sphere where popular-democratic struggles are grouped together – race, gender, age, community, ethnicity, nation and so forth' (2000, p.45).

Civil society is traditionally where community and voluntary organizations, or what are collectively termed as the 'third sector', have been located. The three sectors being:

- the business private sector, which is 'privately' owned and profit motivated;

- the public sector, owned by the state, discussed here as the statutory sector involved in civic activities;

- the third sector, the social economy, including a wide range of community, voluntary and not-for-profit activities.

However, civil society as well as referring to particular types of groups and organizations is identified as an independent setting for specific activities. For example, Walzer (1995) sees civil society as 'the space of uncoerced human association and also the set of relational networks – formed for the sake of family, faith, interest, and ideology – that fill this space' (1995, p.7). It is therefore an important independent space for the type of critical dialogue discussed in Chapter 2, a public sphere which provides spaces in which differences can be debated and taken forward (Johnston, 2008).

The area of **civic** interaction is not usually referred to as a society, but as the sphere where government and the delivery of its services takes place, including the discharging of rights and responsibilities of citizens, and where citizenship duties in relation to democratic involvement are carried out (civic being derived from the Latin *civis*, citizen).

The involvement of citizens in these activities is usually referred to as civic engagement. This involves public participation in the process of governance and democratic structures and processes, and the development of active and empowered communities which facilitates and implements local and national policy-making.

To help analyse the relationship between the worker, participant or community group and civic and civil involvement, the following types of power and their application can be used:

1. Delegated power and authority such as in representative democracies. Here power is held by elected people. However, elections may only happen once every four years and may involve a small number of voters. This type of civic society leads through consensus.

2. Empowered citizens, referred to as participatory democracy, with ongoing involvement in decision making, which should support and refresh (1).

3. Collective power through shared social spaces (civil).

4. An amalgamation of one to three above.

The differing relationships between the civil and civic spheres has been explored in research by the University of Bristol (Howard, 2008) with communities in Bulgaria, Nicaragua and Britain. Their work has shown that there is an often an interdependence between the civic and civil sectors within societies. In Bulgaria and former communist countries there had been a very controlling state or civic sector, with little room for other organizations in the civil sector. In the UK, the state and third sector have been interdependent, the state often financing third sector organizations. Nicaragua is an example of a country with a vibrant and independent civil sector, providing popular, participatory spaces, which were autonomous, creative and politicized, and where grass roots organizations such as social movements and campaigning pressure groups were located.

The research, although showing the differing relationships between the state (civic) and the third sector (civil society), showed a trend towards a loss of autonomy of the civil sphere and an adoption of the work of the state in all three countries. Any opposition to government priorities from third sector organizations resulted in a loss of state funding.

It is therefore important that we consider the implications of government social policy and the impact that it has on civil society, and the implications for our role as workers enabling critical dialogue and change.

Social policy, active citizenship, the third sector and the role of the state

Social policy interventions relating to the focus of this book are currently falling within three related but potentially opposing and contradictory themes that will be discussed below. The areas of government intervention exacerbate the dilemmas for professional Youth and Community Workers, particularly in relation to their role supporting the civil sphere of activities, for example with volunteers and active citizens. As shown by the Bristol research discussed above, this overview will show that the government is making strategic interventions into the lives of the community and community organizations (civil society/the third sector) in a way not previously known in the United Kingdom.

In 2003 David Blunkett identified the key government themes as being 'a shared belief in the power of education to enrich the minds of citizens, a commitment to develop a mutually supportive relationship amongst the members of a democratic community and a determination to strengthen citizens' role in shaping the public realm' (Home Office, 2003, p.3)'. He further identified the government role in trying to achieve these aims by stating 'instead of standing back and letting go of the values of solidarity, mutuality and democratic self determination, government – both central and local – has a vital role to play in strengthening community life and renewing civic involvement (Home Office, 2003, p.4).

In the Home Office pamphlet *Active Citizens, Strong Communities – Progressing Civil Renewal* (Home Office, 2003) he made the case that this was an essential task for the development of strong communities and necessary to avoid a fragmented society in the face of new technologies, changing workplace patterns, increased work mobility and increasingly distant managerial structures. The crucial ingredients were strengthened communities, partnerships in meeting public needs and active citizens.

The three social policy strands can be divided into, firstly, work with the third sector and its role in relation to the delivery of services; secondly, work with communities; and thirdly, the role of individual citizens/community members. These approaches are evident in the following social policy areas:

1. A commitment to civil renewal and the development of the third sector through initiatives such as 'Futurebuilders' (Home Office, 2004a), and 'Building Civil Renewal' (Home Office, 2004b).

2. Community engagement in decision making, developing a 'Partnership in Meeting Public Needs' (Home Office, 2003, p.6), for example through 'Together We Can' (Home Office, 2005a) and 'Citizen Engagement and Public Services: Why Neighbourhoods Matter' (ODPM, 2005).

3. Active citizenship: 'citizens should be given more opportunity and support to become actively involved in defining and tackling the problem of their communities and improving their quality of life' (Home Office, 2003, p.6), for example, through the ALAC programme (Woodward, 2004), and volunteering programmes designed to develop and share the capacity of individuals, such as 'Youth Matters' (DfES, 2005), and 'V' (2008), a national volunteering programme for 16–25 year olds (www.vinspired.com).

Exploration of these initiatives shows that the first two are primarily aimed at building what Putnam (2000) calls social capital, particularly through the development of a healthy civil and civic society, whereas the third is being used primarily for the development of human capital through the development of individual capacity, and is discussed further in Chapter 4, on the characteristics of volunteering.

In the first strand the Home Office saw 'Building Civil Renewal' as 'a way to empower people in their communities *to provide an answer to our contemporary social problems'* (Home Office, 2004b, p.2) The focus is primarily on the development of community capacity building, which will enable 'people increasingly to do things for themselves *and the state* to facilitate, support and enable citizens to lead self determined, fulfilled lives for the common good' (Home Office, 2004b, p.2). This is to be achieved through support to community and voluntary sector group organizations and networks.

Similarly, in the second strand, the Office of the Deputy Prime Minister (ODPM) document 'Why Neighbourhoods Matter' (2005), followed by the Department of Communities and Local Government's 'Strong and Prosperous Communities' (DCLG, 2006), sets out proposals for organizational change at a local authority and neighbourhood level to enable sustainable improvements in public services and the engagement of citizens with government institutions. 'Why Neighbourhoods Matter' also recognizes the value of volunteering:

> *Voluntary activity in the community is associated with better health, lower crime, improved educational performance and greater life satisfaction. Active involvement in decisions that affect individuals and the places with which they associate can give greater depth to citizenship. (ODPM, 2005, p.9)*

This approach is also evident in 'Aiming High', the ten year strategy for work with young people. It makes clear the government emphasis on rights and responsibilities, that people have a right to have a voice and influence services but in return they have the responsibility to carry out change themselves. The strategy makes clear that 'while young people, parents and communities have the right to excellent quality youth support services, in return, they have a responsibility to get involved in addressing the issues faced by young people and help improve what is on offer' (DfCSF, 2007. Section 1.47).

The influence of communitarianism

The third strand, that of developing community participation and volunteering, has been influenced by the communitarian approach. The leading exponent of communitarianism is Amitai Etzioni. In his work *Spirit of community, rights responsibilities and the communitarian agenda* (1993), he discusses the concept of communitarianism as developing from ancient Greece and the Old and the New Testaments. He states that, 'communitarians call to restore civic virtues, for people to live up to their responsibilities and not merely focus on their entitlements, and to shore up the moral foundations of society' (np). This is a call for the balancing of individualism and social responsibility. For Etzioni there are two cardinal founding principles of communitarianism, the core virtues of the good society as social order (based on moral values) and autonomy. The ideal state, or 'golden rule', is where these two states are in equilibrium (1997).

The influence of these communitarian ideas on government strategy is evident in the report for the National Council for Voluntary Organizations, Civil Renewal and Active Citizenship (Jochum et al., 2005). It identifies underlying themes in relation to government strategies: rights and responsibilities, law and order, targeted geographical communities, social cohesion, community participation, particularly in the public realm (or state), and the development of civil society particularly through the development of the community and voluntary sector.

The second theme, that of community involvement in decision making, was made explicit in the follow up to the government's 'Strong and Prosperous Communities' White Paper (2006), the Local Government and Public Involvement in Health Act 2007 and what has become known as 'the duty to involve', in this case particularly in relation to health services. The Act aims to give a stronger voice to citizens about where they live and the services they receive, to support local leadership and increase the ability for communities to have local demands and needs met. The Act gives local authorities a new duty to 'inform, consult and involve' local people: 'Government wants everyone, irrespective of where they live, work or play, to be provided with opportunities to get involved' (2007, np).

The influence of notions of 'capital'

In addition to the influence of communitarianism, government policy has been influenced by the work of Robert Putnam as articulated in his work *Bowling Alone: The Collapse and Revival of American Community* (2000). Putnam in his analysis of the decline of *civic* involvement in the United States, explores what he describes as a 'dangerous rip tide . . . we have been pulled apart from one another and from our communities over the last third of a century' (2000, p.27). He identifies three types of capital that have been involved in this decline: physical, human and social. 'Whereas physical capital refers to physical objects and human capital refers to properties of individuals, social capital refers to connections among individuals, social networks and the norms of reciprocity and trustworthiness that arise from them' (2000, p.19). Putnam sees social capital as being akin to neighbourliness. He identifies the personal as well as collective benefits, for example through networking, and that the concept has links with the notions of community.

Putnam, however, does not view social capital as being totally positive, and debates the ways in which strong 'in groups' can be exclusive and perpetuate destructive norms. He sees the task as being how 'the positive consequences of social capital (mutual support, cooperation, trust, institutional effectiveness) can be maximized and the negative manifestations (sectarianism, ethnocentrism, corruption), minimized' (2000, p.22). Putnam identifies several possible explanations for the decline in social capital: the change in work pattern, the time and financial resources available to both men and women, the individualization brought about by developing use of technology and the mass media, and attitudinal generational change.

The concerns about such social exclusion and the decline of neighbourliness has been the impetus behind many government community engagement strategies which have placed emphasis on rebuilding social capital, particularly as a way of developing community cohesion. In the Home Office document 'Building Civil Renewal' (2004b) the government defined social capital as 'shared understandings, levels of trust, associational membership and informal networks of human relations that facilitate social exchange and underpin social institutions' (2004b, p.33). Field (2003), in his work on social capital, discussed the advantages of the development of social capital for the state, particularly that of linking (bridging) social capital, for example within communities that may be divided. However, Field argued for governments to 'act as an enabler, and then stand back' (2003, p.134) and further that, 'in developing policies which favour social capital investment, government also needs to avoid the risk of either inadvertently undermining existing sources of social capital, or of producing connections that have more negative than positive consequences' (2003, p.135).

This discussion has identified that the development of social capital, if it is the basis for civil society, has usually been carried out and determined by the members of communities and groups, not instigated and directed by the state and civic institutions. The development of government strategies that strive to control the focus and direction of the processes that create social capital has important implications for our practice, and creates dilemmas for us in relation to our role as empowerer, advocate and enabler for the third sector and civil society. Rather than the state providing welfare, it is now drawing on the constituents of what were elements of independent civil society, the community and voluntary sector, to provide services and carry out activities on the state's behalf. This is apparent in the growing demands for the community, and community and voluntary sector organizations to deliver welfare services (for example, community policing, children and youth services).

A fourth type of capital

Putnam (2000) had not foreseen this trend towards the intrusion of the state in the third sector, and the move towards the community and voluntary sector carrying out what have previously been the roles of the welfare state.

I propose that the concept of state capital be added to Putnam's categories of capital (Packham, 2006), the process of non-statutory organizations within the community and voluntary sector taking on what were previously statutory roles, and so primarily providing benefits for the state as opposed to social capital. Hodgson (2004) uses the term 'manufactured civil society' to refer to 'groups that are formed and funded, at least initially, through some type of state initiative' (2004, p.145). Although referring to large organizations such as Sure Start and Single Regeneration Budget (SRB) schemes, his identification of organizations and activities which are constructed as opposed to organic and community initiated and led has important implications for the voluntary and community sector workers and communities. In Hodgson's view, based on research undertaken with different sizes of groups in Wales, 'where groups are coerced into partnerships by outside influences rather than coming together of their own volition, specific problems can arise which can undermine the values and ethos of civil society and threaten rather than strengthen social capital' (2004, p.157).

Hodgson's term 'manufactured civil society' refers to the process of state intervention within civil society which, I have identified, results in the production of state capital.

> *Civil society has become increasingly utilised in policy initiatives . . . civil society traditionally viewed as a sphere outside of the state, now finds itself engaged in various types of 'partnership' with both the state and the business community. This has had the effect of redrawing the boundaries between civil society and the state. (Hodgson, 2004, p.139)*

This analysis and the inclusion of a fourth type of capital enables a more accurate discussion of the dichotomies and dilemmas faced by professional workers (and volunteers) who are increasingly asked to carry out the requirements of government determined priorities. This trend is counter to the ethos and principles of Youth and Community Work, which has been rooted in a commitment to the self identification of needs and consequent action.

ACTIVITY **3.3**

Using your understanding of human, social and state capital, refer back to Table 3.1 and identify the types of benefit that are being generated by the work of the groups and their members.

Consider whether this would influence your approach to the work of this group. For example, how does the work fit with the principles of your practice? What priority and how much time would you allocate to this work?

CASE STUDY

Enabling 'state' capital? The Active Learning for Active Citizenship (ALAC) pilots

The ALAC programme arose directly as a result of David Blunkett's introduction of citizenship education in schools and trials of a 16–19-year-olds citizenship programme. ALAC was to be a comparable programme for adults to

> *learn the knowledge and skills for active citizenship . . . The development was to be totally complementary to the evolution of the civil renewal agenda and the Together We Can campaign . . . the three interlinked features of civil renewal – active citizenship, strong and prosperous communities and partnership with public bodies. (Woodd, 2007, p.11)*

The ALAC pilot projects worked in seven regions across England with different groups and methods, enabling participants to raise their levels of confidence and awareness so that they could become more active within their communities and where appropriate influence local and national policy and practice. The programme highlighted existing work and developed new areas with the help of the Home Office and the Department for Communities and Local Government funding.

See www.takepart.org for a summary of the methods and work carried out.

However as Putnam (2000) recognized that not all social capital is beneficial (for example bonding and inward looking social capital can be exclusive), similarly it should be recognized that state capital can also have differing types of impact. For simplicity these can be referred to as either generative, or punitive.

In the generative sphere, this is illustrated by the many government schemes which are aiming to empower local communities and involve them in the development of local groups, activities, organizations and decision making, For example, through the local authority compact agreements which negotiate methods and strategies for consultation with community and voluntary groups.

However, other areas of social policy have sought to involve community members in implementing surveillance and crime and disorder strategies, and so have created punitive state capital. Examples include involving community members as community wardens; voluntary groups being financially coerced to obtain funds by working with named young offenders; and asylum seekers undertaking community service in order to obtain food or accommodation (Asylum and Immigration Act, Home Office, 2004d).

These state capital engendered strategies can work positively, but it depends on the degree to which all community members have control over their involvement and are encouraged to be involved in true critical dialogue as opposed to tokenistic consultation.

Table 3.2 Types of capital

	Social Capital	Human Capital	State Capital
Negative consequences	Bonding – tight group identity excluding others	Individualized – focus on self development – employability	Punitive – support and funding used to control and monitor
Positive consequences	Bridging – outward looking, neighbourly.	Engaged – working with others to bring about change	Generative – involvement assists in community development, self help.

As Table 3.2 above shows, all types of capital can have positive and negative consequences. For example, the involvement of community members as citizens in predominantly state-controlled activities is problematic if the space for independent and critical discussion is thereby reduced. Therefore, the role for workers is to enable their own, as well as the citizens' agency and voice. Similarly the role of the community and voluntary sector which primarily supports individual volunteers has seen its role in independent civil society challenged particularly by the development of the state. This has placed such organizations in a contradictory position, at times welcoming the recognition and funding for the work, at others bemoaning the restrictions placed by target driven, funding led bureaucracy. As Davies states when discussing the period from the 1960s, 'more and more . . . these organizations in effect became clients of the state, as locally and nationally, they came to rely on public funds to develop or even just maintain their core facilities and activities', and particularly in the 1980s when the Thatcher government insisted that 'they adjust their programmes to fit ministerial objectives' (1999, p.186).

CASE STUDY

Developing social capital: the Refugee Charter

Refugee Charter for Manchester

Define us not by our differences but by the principles we share

We are people of courage, ingenuity and perseverance who have been forced to come to seek refuge in Manchester.

We are refugees and asylum seekers, exercising our legal right under the 1951 UN Convention to seek safety from persecution in our countries of origin. We include families, lone individuals, men women and children, young and old, people with disabilities and unaccompanied minors.

We applaud and thank all individuals, public agencies and organizations who have welcomed us and supported us to re-build our lives in the UK.

However the current situation for many asylum seekers and refugees is critical. We see our communities increasingly marginalised, denied or unable to access employment with, limited and problematic access to health services and dispersed to highly deprived areas where individuals are isolated, vulnerable and subject to harassment and physical attacks.

While refugees and asylum seekers have different entitlements under British law, we ask that the rights in the law be upheld and that our basic, universal human rights be respected. Immigration policies often run contrary to other government objectives including reducing rough sleeping, encouraging employment and creating an inclusive society.

We exert all possible effort to positively contribute and integrate with our host communities. There is a long history of refugees and migrants making a significant contribution to the life of the city, and current refugees must be recognized as continuing this contribution.

Integration is a dynamic and two way process, placing a demand on receiving societies and the new communities.

In order for us to rebuild our lives and fully integrate into society we call for:

Basic Rights

1. Recognition of the inherent dignity and equal and inalienable rights of all members of the human family as the foundation of freedom, justice and peace;

2. Especially vulnerable members of refugee communities to be treated with the same care and respect as those from host communities expect and where children are involved, the rights of the child must be paramount;

3. Appropriate provisions to be made for refugees and asylum seekers with special needs, such as unaccompanied minors and disabled refugees and asylum seekers;

4. Service providers within Manchester to recognize that they have a responsibility to ensure that all refugee policies are compassionate, ethically sound and consistent with international legal standards;

5. Recognition of the right to adequate legal representation to enable us to have a fair and just asylum hearing;

6. Recognition of the crucial importance of advice and interpretation services in enabling us to realise our rights and contribute to our host community;

Healthcare

7. Recognition that we should have the same access to healthcare as our host community;

8. Asylum seekers and refugees with mental health needs to have these met appropriately and sensitively and to promote good mental health in acknowledgement of the fact that many of us have been traumatised in our country of origin and that our lives are still stressful and uncertain;

Housing

9. The right to safe, appropriate accommodation. This should be suitably located, well managed, in good repair and with adequate support to enable us to resettle and rebuild our homes;

10. The recognition that enforced destitution is an inhumane policy which is harmful and dangerous for the victims and damaging for the host communities;

Education

11. Schools and colleges to encourage integration through valuing each child regardless of background and recognising that each child and young person can play a fundamental role in educating others and promoting greater understanding of the issues affecting refugees;

12. Recognition of the emotional needs of refugee children and the importance of a stable and safe environment in order to assist in their development;

13. Appropriate provision to allow adult learners to access education, especially ESOL courses;

Employment

14. Recognition that we want to work, and have no desire to become an economic burden, and that current legislation, which prevents asylum seekers from working, has a detrimental effect both on the individuals concerned and the city as a whole and on community cohesion and integration;

15. Encouragement and promotion of full scale participation in employment preparation and personal development for asylum seekers;

16. Encouragement and promotion of appropriate training and employment opportunities for refugees to enable them to participate in the economic, social and cultural life of the city;

Community Cohesion and Social bonds

17. Respect as law-abiding people who should not be suspected or accused of a crime due to our immigration status;

18. The right to live in safety without fear of persecution or physical attacks from racist abusers;

19. Recognition that irresponsible media coverage hurts real people and that media representation should therefore be sensitive, fair and truthfully reflective of the positive contribution we make to our host community; and

20. Support for our community organisations and refugee organisations to increase peoples' confidence and ability to integrate on equal terms, to promote respect for the cultures, arts and languages that we bring and to increase inter-cultural understanding.

An example of a facilitated process which has developed social capital, although funded through the government sponsored ALAC programme, is the development of the Refugee Charter in Manchester.

Representatives of groups of refugees and asylum seekers were facilitated through the Freirian (1972) model of a 'School of Participation' (delivered in partnership between Church Action on Poverty and Manchester Refugee Support Network and Community Pride) to come together to identify (problem pose) an issue that they wanted to discuss (through critical dialogue and praxis) and to change. The group spent several weeks analysing the requirement for better informed and sensitive services, and the causes of their concerns at an individual, community, societal and global level. As a result they identified action that should be taken together, which led to the drawing up of the Refugee Charter. The charter was widely publicized and disseminated throughout Manchester and launched formally in the Town Hall. The participants in the programme were enabled to reflect on the process of the group, their learning and what had been achieved and still needed to be carried out, the process of transformation. As a result of their work, services were better informed, contributing to state capital, but importantly the participants had been empowered through their networking and the increase in their knowledge and skills.

The essential difference between this and the case study of the generation of state capital outlined above (the ALAC pilots) is that the participants had control of the process of the activity throughout, with the worker acting as an enabling facilitator.

The development of capital and the role of the individual

The importance being placed by government on the role of volunteers is evident in the development of the Communities and Local Government Empowerment White Paper (2008). The benefits the government sees in citizen involvement, and different types of volunteering, are clearly set out in the consultation document.

Government has an interest in promoting active citizenship across the spectrum because:

- it will enable people and communities to find common solutions to shared problems;

- it can generate 'social capital' – bonding, bridging and linking;

- it can stimulate collective efficacy – social pressure on groups of people to behave responsibly and to look out for each others' interest;

- it can achieve 'co-production' – government working alongside the third sector to achieve shared outcomes in public services;

- there can be clear progression routes along the spectrum into forms of civic involvement which support democratic and public service infrastructure' (DCLG, 2008, p.15).

However, when considering the White Paper along with other government volunteering initiatives their approaches can be see to raise dilemmas for Youth and Community Workers who are working with such active citizens and volunteers.

Firstly, the government emphasis has primarily been focused on the individual and the development of their human capital. This is opposed to developing volunteers as collective citizens (Storrie, 2004) who are aware of their role in groups, as part of teams or involved in forms of association. As Hodgson states, when discussing the government's focus on voluntary activity, it is seen 'as a means through which skills are acquired and developed, personal self confidence enhanced and training for work provided' (2004, p.141).

Secondly, volunteering is often being used in a punitive and compulsory manner, which puts the interest of the state and the generation of state capital to the fore, and threatens the nature of voluntary activity. As Field states, 'policies designed to promote individuals inevitably end up degrading the meaning of volunteering, as the existence of inducements removes the element of altruism and channels people into doing something more out of self-interest than from a desire to serve others' (Field, 2003 p.119).

Thirdly, those being encouraged to be active citizens and community leaders may be implementing government programmes and taking on the delivery of services as discussed above. As stated in the report by the National Council for Voluntary Organizations, the government is 're-engaging citizens with decision making processes and sharing risks and responsibilities between citizens and state' (Jochum et al. 2005, p.21). As a result volunteers are becoming an 'instrument of government rather than a force for change' (2005, p.9) through collective action.

Fourthly, as indicated by Jochum, the government's emphasis on volunteering is removing the potential for volunteers to be part of active groups of citizens involved in social change. As Jochum states, the 'government's attention is how citizens relate to the state and its institutions rather than how they might relate to each other' (Jochum et al., 2005, p.11). This represents a move away from the initial intention of the Blunkett approach to civil renewal, where he stated, 'there is a danger that people will cease to function as citizens altogether and society will fragment into individuals who look only to themselves and their private circle of friends and relatives . . . citizens in general need to realize that their personal interests are best safeguarded when they actively take part in the protection of their common good' (2003, pp.4–6). The types of volunteers and their contribution to human, social and state capital are discussed in detail in Chapter 4.

The blurring of roles of volunteers and their function is problematic as it challenges the independent nature of social capital within civil society, and poses important questions for Youth and Community Workers who are involved with either individuals as volunteers or active citizens. Some volunteers with whom we work may put self interest before social benefit, whilst others, who may be termed active citizens, such as those who are part of the ALAC programme, are primarily involved in voluntary activity for community or group benefit. Here the role of the worker could be seen as encouraging the development of state capital through active citizenship and civil renewal activities and so predominantly to enable a more efficient state. Alternatively our role could be to support and enable activities engendering social capital and vibrant creative, independent communities.

The discussion above recognizes that the notion of social capital is problematic. However, it aims to identify that current government initiatives are potentially omitting important elements of informal education and community development: that of space for deliberation in groups, and community self help and determination.

Conclusion

This chapter has discussed the government approach to the development of civic and civil engagement of citizens and highlighted some of the contradictions and subsequent dilemmas for those working within this sector.

The main development during the life of the current Labour government has been its intervention into sectors which were previously independent. The government has recognized the significant role of the third sector and by its approach has given more consideration to its relationship with this sector than any previous government, those that ignored its role altogether and previous Labour governments who saw the state's role to take over many of the third sector's functions. However, the government has not sought to support the existing independent role of the third sector. Rather it has sought to influence and control it, and use community and voluntary organizations as a deliverer of its services. Consequently this has placed restrictions on the sector's autonomy and creativity.

In relation to citizens, the government has become involved in areas which were usually determined by individual citizens. Through the development of volunteering, much of which is no longer freely chosen (for example as part of the school citizenship curriculum or activity undertaken as part of a community service order), and through the development of a set curriculum for active citizenship, the government can be seen to be seeking to control the role of individuals in civic and civil society.

The Active Learning for Active Citizenship programme initiated by the Home Office is an example of the tensions and contradictions apparent in much of the social policy initiatives discussed here. The impetus for the ALAC report came from David Blunkett who is an advocate of communitarian ideals. However, his methods for engendering engagement within society were primarily focused on the development of civic duty. His draft citizenship curriculum reflected this. The tensions apparent through the ALAC programme have been that the government seems to take a primarily civic approach to citizenship. It has a focus on individual/human capital through the training of community leaders, although it does not see these as volunteers, and although working through the community and voluntary sector, it fails to recognize the need to increase the capacity of these groups as opposed to individuals. The ALAC pilots critiqued these approaches and identified the importance of civil as well as civic engagement and the importance of association of the participants, and learning and working as groups and the importance of community action by groups and organizations as opposed to isolated leaders.

The debates in this chapter and the illustrations of practice have illustrated that there can be a partnership between the civil and civic areas of society, where each complements and informs the other whilst retaining their separate roles and functions. For example, 'community activity is essentially autonomous and therefore complementary to more systematic democratic systems' (Woodward, 2004, p.10). The discussions have identified the production of human, social and state capital as the outcome of civic and civil involvement.

It is essential that as workers we recognize, create and support spaces where independent deliberation and action can take place, and as Batsleer states:

> *It is important to recognize that all critical practice . . . starts by being implicated in the social policy discourses which surround (young) people. There is no alternative but to struggle with the discourses in order to recognize their impact, value the resources they offer but also and where necessary, to devise ways and means of countering their negative constructions of (young) people and their potential. (Batsleer, 2008, p.55)*

Youth and Community Workers therefore have an important role as informal educators with those involved in civic and civil activities, to enable participants to think critically about how best to spend their time and, as discussed in relation to human, social and state capital, identify who will benefit and how.

REFERENCES

Batsleer, J (2008) *Informal education with young people*. London: Sage.

Davies, B (1999) *A history of the youth service in England.* Leicester: Youth Work Press.

Department of Communities and Local Government (DLCG) (2007) *Local Government and Public Involvement in Health Act*. London: DLCG.

Department of Communities and Local Government (DLGC) (2008) *The community power pack* (consultation on the Empowerment White Paper*).* London: DLCG.

Department for Education and Skills, (2005) *Youth matters, Green Paper, consultation document.* London: HMSO, DFES.

Department for Schools Children and Families (DfCSF) (2007) *Aiming high.* London: DfCFS/HM Treasury.

Edwards, M (2005) *Civil society.* London: Polity Press.

Etzioni, A (1993) *The spirit of community, rights responsibilities and the communitarian agenda.* London: Fontana Press.

Etzioni, A (1995) *The spirit of community: The reinvention of american society.* New York: Touchstone.

Etzioni, A (1997) *The new golden rule: Community and morality in a democratic society.* New York: Basic Books.

Field, J (2003) *Social capital.* London: Routledge.

Hodgson, L (2004) Manufactured civil society: Counting the cost: *Critical Social Policy*, 79, 24 (2): 139–164. London: Sage.

Home Office (HO), (Blunkett, D) (2003) *Active citizens, strong communities – progressing civil renewal.* London: Home Office.

Home Office (HO) (2004a) *Futurebuilders.* Active Communities Directorate, Home Office. London: TSO.

Home Office (HO) (2004b) *Building civil renewal*. Civil Renewal Unit, Home Office. London: TSO.

Home Office (HO) (2004c) *Asylum and Immigration (Treatment of Claimants) Act.* London: TSO.

Home Office (2005a) *Together we can.* Civil Renewal Unit, Home Office. London: TSO.

Howard, J (2008) State/civil society relations in Bulgaria, Nicaragua, England and Wales, paper to Here the People Decide Conference, Bradford 31/1/2008. Bristol: University of the West of England.

Jochum, V, Pratten, B and Wilding, K (2005) *Civil Renewal and active citizenship: a guide to the debate.* A report from the National Council for Voluntary Organizations. London: NCVO.

Johnston, R (2008) Re-viewing the Active Learning for Active Citizenship Model, in J Annette and M Mayo, eds, *Active learning for active citizenship*. Nottingham: NIACE.

Office of the Deputy Prime Minister (ODPM) (2005) *Citizen engagement and public services: Why neighbourhoods matter*. London: ODPM.

Packham, C (2006) Doing us out of a job? EdD thesis, Manchester Metropolitan University.

Popple, K (2000) *Analysing community work. Its theory and practice.* Buckingham: Open University Press.

Prochaska, F (2002) *Schools of citizenship: charity and civic virtue.* London: Civitas.

Putnam, RD (2000) *Bowling alone: The collapse and revival of American community*. New York: Simon and Schuster.

Storrie, T (2004) Citizens or what?, in J Roche, ed., *Youth in society*. London: Sage: pp.52–60.

Walzer, M (1995) The concept of a civil society, in M Walzer ed. *Toward a global civil society*. Providence, RI: Berghahn Books, pp.7–27.

Woodd, C (2007) Active learning for active citizenship: The policy context. *OR Insight*, 20 (2): 8–12.

Woodward, V (2004) *Active learning for active citizenship*. Civil Renewal Unit. London: Home Office.

Chapter 4
Volunteers and active citizens

This chapter will provide information and activities to help you understand the complexity of different types of volunteers. It will enable you to meet the community development occupational standards, specifically in relation to working with communities to collectively bring about social change and justice by 'identifying their needs, opportunities rights and responsibilities'.

The values and principles of community development are specifically considered here in relation to enabling a 'self determination environment', particularly in relation to 'valuing the concerns or issues that communities identify as their starting points' and 'raising awareness of the range of choices open to them'. When considering the complex nature of volunteering this chapter meets the standards of enabling 'sustainable communities' by 'promoting the empowerment of individuals and communities' (Department for Communities and Local Government (DCLG), 2006a, pp.47–48).

ACTIVITY **4.1**

To enable you to understand fully the complex nature of volunteering discussed in this chapter, first write down three characteristics of volunteers. Now use these three characteristics to form the basis of a definition of what is a volunteer.

A volunteer is someone who . . .

You may have written something like: a volunteer is someone who decides to get involved; who is learning a skill so that they can move on; who does work for nothing. The definition of volunteer, their types and what is achieved by volunteering will be discussed in this chapter.

What is a volunteer? Frameworks for locating types of volunteer

Whilst Youth and Community Work is now seen as a paid profession, there is a long tradition of volunteering by either carrying out work within communities or by work to support voluntary activity. Volunteering has therefore been an important element of work and wider society. Voluntarists, those who engage in voluntary activity, have been seen by some as 'a great army of busy bodies' who 'were the active people of England and provided the ground swell of her history' (Taylor, 1965, p.175).

Government schemes to encourage volunteering such as the Russell Commission on Youth Action and Engagement (2005), use the United Nations definition of volunteering (2001):

> *There are three key defining characteristics of volunteering. First the activity should not be undertaken primarily for financial reward, although the reimbursement of expenses and some token payment can be allowed. Second the activity should be undertaken voluntarily, according to an individual's own free will, although there are grey areas here too, such as school community service schemes which encourage, and sometimes require, students to get involved in voluntary work and Food for Work programmes, where there is an explicit exchange between community involvement and food assistance. Third, the activity should be of benefit to someone other than the volunteer, or to society at large, although it is recognized that volunteering brings benefit to the volunteer as well.*

> *Within this broad conceptual framework it is possible to identify at least four different types of volunteer activity: mutual aid or self help: philanthropy or service to others, participation or civic engagement, and advocacy or campaigning. Each of these parts occurs in all parts of the world. (Russell Commission, 2005, p.4)*

Volunteers have existed throughout history, and at different times the four elements identified in the United Nations definition have had different degrees of prominence. Prochaska (2002) traces the development of what he terms 'charity' and philanthropy in an English context. He identifies that in the Victorian period most Victorians thought voluntary activity and charitable activity 'to be the most wholesome way of promoting individual reformation and social harmony' (2002, p.2), whereas he sees the current volunteering initiatives and notions of charity being predominantly philanthropic, such as the giving of financial or physical resources.

ACTIVITY 4.2

Think about an organization you have been involved with or you know about that involves volunteering. This could be for a particular activity or on a regular basis.

For example a community association may have a parent and toddler group each week that involves local parents as volunteers to help run the activities. They may also organize a large community festival once a year which involves a large numbers of volunteers, to plan and run the event.

Make a list of five of the volunteers (use initials or their role/job) and using the table below list the outcomes and achievements of their volunteering.

Volunteer (use initial/ job title)	Skills contributed/ shared	Knowledge contributed/shared	Outcome/ what achieved
Example: CP Treasurer on Management Committee	Some computing, funding bids, dealings with accountants and funders	Experience of community organizations and local community, some national policy understanding	Support to workers, enables some project development. Information to management committee, suggestions for financial direction etc.
1			
2			
3			
4			
5			

Volunteers, what they contribute/share and outcomes/what is achieved

Despite criticisms of volunteering as being a form of 'cheap labour', a substitute for professional intervention, or patronizing 'do gooding', it can be seen from Activity 4.2, that there are benefits for the individual volunteer, group and community.

Charitable, voluntary activity has been seen by commentators such as Putnam (2000), Etzioni (1995, 1997) and Prochaska (2002) as an important element of civic and civil society. Civil society, as evidenced through the activities of voluntary organizations, serves an important function as an intermediary between the people and the state. For example, Putnam, when advocating a communitarian agenda, states 'volunteering is a part of the syndrome of good citizenship and political involvement, not an alternative to it' (2000, p.132).

Historically, the status of volunteering has changed depending on the role of the state in relation to welfare, volunteering and philanthropic activity, being at its height in the period before the development of the welfare state in England. The present government interest in volunteering can be analysed in relation to how the role and function of volunteering is viewed. The New Labour government has continued the Thatcherite reduction of the 'collectivist' welfare state, with the consequent reduction in dependence on a centralized welfare system. The government has moved to the 'Third Way' approach, identifying and developing the ground between state and society with an increased role for the private and third sector (the third sector being organizations and groups in the voluntary and not for profit sector, for example charities, local groups and social enterprises (see www.thirdsector.co.uk, June 2007). This will be further discussed in Chapter 5, which explores the government involvement in civic and civil involvement.

The current expansion in volunteering can be viewed as

- a way to enable community members to be contributing social citizens in relation to their communities, i.e. civil engagement; for example the Russell Commission states 'young volunteers are making a positive contribution to the lives of others, and are helping to strengthen the fabric of our communities' (2004, p.1);

- a means of enabling community organization and self help (which could be viewed as counter to democratic and centralized systems);

- contributing to local and national decision making through democratic civic structures, e.g. as school governors;

- self interest and the development of individual experience, skills and knowledge;

- an increasingly compulsory and punitive activity.

The reasons for volunteering and the implications for the worker are discussed in Chapter 4. However, the different types of volunteer need to be recognized so that their contribution can be enhanced.

Category of volunteer and level of skill and knowledge

In line with the recognition that there are different types of volunteers, I have used a framework that draws on the work of Dreyfus and Dreyfus's (1980) model of skill acquisition, to identify the different types of volunteer, particularly with regard to their existing skill and knowledge with regard to the tasks they are undertaking.

Table 4.1 Category of volunteer and level of skill and knowledge (from Dreyfus and Dreyfus, 1980)

Novice, an unskilled/inexperienced volunteer

Advanced beginner, possessing some skill and knowledge in limited areas

Competent, more skilled, able to plan consciously, application of longer term goals

Proficient, able to act quickly as effective co-worker, showing sensitivity and skill

Expert, high levels of proficiency both skills and knowledge of value to the agency

ACTIVITY 4.3

Thinking about the group of five volunteers which you analysed in Activity 4.2, list them in the table below in relation to their degrees of expertise.

Volunteer (give initials and role)	Type in relation to Table 4.1	Explain why you have chosen this type
Example: CP, project treasurer	Novice	Knows nothing about accounting!
Volunteer 1		
Volunteer 2		
Volunteer 3		
Volunteer 4		
Volunteer 5		

How useful do you think this type of analysis is? Are people always one type of volunteer or might they be an expert in relation to one type of activity or setting and a novice in another? Do people always stay in the type you have identified?

Volunteers may move along the expert to novice spectrum based on their own capacity, familiarity with the setting, and the work to be undertaken. An expert could therefore mean someone possessing a lot of local knowledge: this is more likely to be the case with people working with their own community. It might, therefore, be predicted that a young person undertaking fund raising for the first time may have a greater need for support than an accountant assisting as treasurer on a management committee. However, more detailed analysis will show that this volunteer type framework does not recognize the complexity of the volunteer involvement. For example, the young fundraiser may have local contacts so would be able to work within the community, and the accountant may have expertise in accounting but lack familiarity with the group and their aims and methods.

To enable an analysis of the types of voluntary activity in relation to the purpose of the work undertaken and resulting benefits, Putnam (2000) and Dewey's (1916) notions of 'doing with' and 'doing for' can be applied. Putnam (2000) discussed how the category of 'doing for' was altruistic as opposed to self help focused. He argues that 'doing with' is part of what he calls social capital and refers to the value of 'networks of social connection' (2000, p.117), and the subsequent 'norms and reciprocity and trustworthiness that arise from them' (2000, p.19). Contrastingly, 'doing for' 'is doing good *for* other people' (2000, p.117) and may not be part of a social network and the resultant benefits and is therefore not viewed by him as being part of social capital. In the same way that human and physical capital contributes towards productivity 'so too social contacts affect the productivity of individuals and groups' (2000, p.117). The divisions between human and social capital are tenuous but might explain the distinction between people who are predominately 'doing for', that is, who are altruistic and may be involved out of self interest, and those who are ' doing with' and engaging in a process of shared community benefit, such as community activists or active citizens.

The considerations in Table 4.1 can be related to the 'doing with' and 'doing for' types of volunteers. A volunteer who is involved within their community may have low levels of technical expertise but may have local knowledge, which may enable their inclusion, whereas someone who is doing for may have neither local knowledge nor skills, which may lead to greater levels of exclusion. It cannot, however, be assumed that 'outsiders' or those 'doing for' cannot be included within communities of action. They may have shared identities with the 'host community', for example as a woman volunteer volunteering with a women's project, and or have levels of expertise which are highly valued by the host group. For example, coMMUni, Manchester Metropolitan University volunteering project, recorded high levels of requests from community groups for volunteers with ICT and mother tongue expertise.

Volunteering and active citizenship

The above discussion has shown that the Dreyfus and Dreyfus's (1980) model is over-simplistic and needs to take into account factors such as the engagement of the volunteer within their community, their motivation and the outcomes in relation to themselves, the community and the state. In order to help locate the type of involvement of unpaid individuals within the community, it is possible to locate them on spectrums of community engagement and individual benefit.

Volunteering and active citizenship can be placed on a similar spectrum to reflect their engagement with 'doing with' and 'for', and opportunities for association and critical dialogue, and the type of capital engendered (as evident in the associated benefit).

Table 4.2 sets out a framework based on the distinctions made by current social policy with regard to the involvement of 'volunteers'. The aim of drawing up the framework is to help clarify the complex nature of the involvement of volunteers, and to recognize the different types of benefits that result from their involvement. The table also helps analyse where there are areas of contention, for example when the volunteer may be primarily engaged for their own or the state's benefit, and to start to indicate what the role of any paid workers might be, for example in relation to any support or training requirements.

The categories used in the framework to aid analysis have been chosen drawing on the theoretical perspectives of 'doing with' and 'for' (Dewey, 1916 and Putnam, 2002); the space to engage in critical dialogue (Freire, 1972), summarized here as association; and identifying who benefits from the activity, either primarily the individual or the community. In addition the outcomes of the volunteering activity are classified in relation to types of capital, drawing on Putnam's (2000) categories. 'Social', relating to community and group capital, that is the components of civil society, 'human' primarily individual capital, and 'state' (Packham, 2006), referring to acting on behalf or in conjunction with the state, or civic engagement.

Putnam in his book *'Bowling alone: the collapse and revival of American community'* (2000) explores what is required to enable the reweaving of the fabric of our communities. He identified three categories of capital involved in modern societies: physical capital which refers to physical objects; human capital which refers to properties of individuals; and social capital which referred to 'connections among individuals, social networks and the norms of reciprocity and trustworthiness that arise from them' (2000, p.19). He argues that social capital and the elements involved in it has value in the same way that human and physical capital contributes towards productivity. Putnam identifies that human capital consists of 'tools and training that enhance individual productivity' (2000, p.18). This definition is reflected in more recent trends in government sponsored volunteering which for many people is seen primarily as being of individual value. This was evidenced in the Year of the Volunteer promotional material which promoted volunteering as 'polishing your CV, improving your skills and self-confidence, meeting new and interesting people and if helping out in the local community isn't enough of an incentive, there are even health benefits associated with volunteering' (www.yearofthevolunteer.org.).

Government initiatives appear to have distinguished between voluntary activity and active citizenship. Volunteering approaches primarily see volunteers in relation to the development of personal capacities, preparedness for work, and as individual citizens. This is opposed to developing volunteers as collective citizens (Storrie, 2004) who are aware of their role in groups, as part of teams or involved in forms of association. As Hodgson (2004) states, when discussing the government's focus on voluntary activity, it is seen 'as a means through which skills are acquired and developed, personal self confidence enhanced and training for work provided' (2004, p.141). I have termed 'state' capital the development of types of volunteering activity involved in the work of the state, and civil society, or as part of government social policy.

Table 4.2 Volunteer types – levels of individual community engagement

Role	With or for	Association	Benefit	Capital
Volunteer	For	Limited	Individual	Human/state
Voluntary assistance	Both	In part	Individual/community	Human/social
Active citizen	Both	In part	Community/individual	Human/social/state
Self help	With	High	Individual/community	Human/social
Community activist	With	High	Community/individual	Social/human

Within this framework, *volunteers* are taken to be people who have become involved in carrying out work of an unpaid nature through schemes designed to link volunteering opportunities to individual skills and requirements, and to enhance their own performance (Hodgson, 2004). An example of this would be university students and staff, and work based volunteering projects. Although of some social benefit the work is primarily carried out for the volunteers' benefit and they have little involvement with the community either through association or residence. This type of involvement through government initiated schemes produces primarily human and state capital as an outcome. The main beneficiaries are the individual but it also meets the predetermined aims of the government initiative.

The category of *voluntary assistance* refers to informal volunteering arrangements, or altruistic actions that are made within neighbourhoods and communities, which would often not be recognized as volunteering, but whose existence has been recognized as valuable for social cohesion and social capital (Putnam, 2000). Such volunteers carry out the work often out of 'neighbourliness' (Harris, 2004), but these may be part of informal reciprocal arrangements. Volunteers may or may not live within the area and do not see their actions as part of community activity. They therefore are only partly involved 'with', and may have limited association. The prevalence of this category of voluntary assistance is supported by the sample data for the Citizenship Survey 2005 (DCLG, 2006b) which showed that 68 per cent of the respondents said that they volunteered informally (as individuals) at least once in the last 12 months. In relation to notions of capital, voluntary assistance as part of an informal arrangement is not part of any government programme, but is primarily carried out for mutual benefit. It therefore contributes to individual, human and social capital.

Active citizens within Table 4.2 are not classed here as volunteers, as they have some distinguishing characteristics. Government initiatives intend that they should be part of the community in which they are active. However, they may or may not be involved in association with that community at a horizontal level. They may also have their own as well as the communities' benefit as a priority, as it is possible that their work may be paid. This type of active citizenship is apparent through the work of the Scarman Trust, a British infrastructure support organization that works at a local level to 'encourage a culture of active citizenship by building the power of ordinary people', what they call 'can-doers'.

As the *self help* category implies, the volunteer will be involved within their community and has become involved as a result of a desire to improve their own circumstances. They are therefore 'doing with'; they will be acting with other people so their levels of association will be high. Although there will be benefits for the community their main aim is for individual benefit. In relation to outcomes they will therefore contribute to human and social capital. Saturday schools that have been set up and staffed by volunteers to meet the perceived lack of positive, culturally specific education for children are an example of this type of volunteer activity. Many such self help initiatives are being supported by small government grants, such as those for children and young people through the Local Network Fund and via local authorities, for example with grants for Neighbours Days' events.

The final category in Table 4.2 is termed *community activist*, akin to that used by Popple (2000) of community action. Within this category the community member is engaged within their community to undertake work, usually based on self identified needs, and is involved with other community members. This type of activity has high levels of association and the main aim is for community benefit. Although producing human capital, the primary outcome is in the development of a healthy and independent third sector, their activity contributing to the development of social capital. This type of activity quite often generates social movements and critiques of government intervention and policies. Therefore, the community activist may not be contributing to the generation of state capital.

It is clear that people may move within the five categories indicated in Table 4.2, and Storrie (2004) suggests that some individuals may undertake what he calls an apprenticeship where people who may be involved as individual citizens 'require contextualization over time in the social and sociable rhythms, rich in democratic moments' (2004, p.58) and then become what he terms collective citizens. This process would equate to a move within the categories in Table 4.2 from involvement with low levels of association to that of high levels, with growing levels of social as opposed to mainly human capital as the outcome.

The Dreyfus and Dreyfus (1980) model can therefore be combined with the elements of the volunteer/activist framework (Table 4.2). This entails discussion of where they are placed in relation to their levels of association, whether they are 'doing with', or 'for' and what their work is primarily achieving in relation to social, human and state capital.

For the purpose of this analysis I will define 'expert' as someone who meets the skills and knowledge that are required to undertake work with high levels of proficiency and value to the agency (Dreyfus and Dreyfus, 1980). This implies that the idea of expert can be context specific and that more importantly it can be locally defined. The notion of expert in itself is not sufficient to make that role adequate in all contexts and settings. I am making the case that what makes it appropriate and useful is if it is coupled with being context specific, and has an understanding of the norms and requirements of that context or setting. I am taking the latter characteristics as being most likely if the person is undertaking work within their own community.

CASE STUDY

Analysis of a team of volunteers undertaking a participatory evaluation

As part of the MMU coMMUni volunteering project a group of six volunteers were facilitated to undertake participatory research into what enabled effective volunteering (Packham et al., 2004). The team all came from voluntary organizations in Tameside, Lancashire, a diverse urban area with a larger than average Bangladeshi population (1.2 per cent compared to 0.6 per cent national average 2001 Census). Using the frameworks identified above (Table 4.1, adapted from Dreyfus and Dreyfus) and the volunteer type framework (Table 4.2) the involvement of the different volunteers and their contributions is discussed. The team was composed of one white woman (N), an Asian woman (F), two white men (B and M) and two Asian men (R and Z). At the end of the participatory evaluation project the team were asked to evaluate the process and their own involvement. Some of their comments are included.

N, as a result of her experience, was 'proficient'. In relation to community engagement she was external to the community in many respects: she was a young white woman, working in a predominantly Asian community. She was, however, highly regarded by members of local community groups with whom she had previously worked successfully, facilitating local groups to meet their own needs. She was therefore involved with work 'for' the community but was involved in relatively high levels of association, mainly at an organization and group level rather than community. She was achieving social capital for an agency predominately involved in state capital, but she also was interested in developing her human capital as was evident by her departure from the agency for a higher status job, acquired as a result of her developing expert status.

M had become involved as a 'competent' participant in the team, he was able to organize and undertake work with minimal support from the worker. He was supported to undertake increasingly responsible tasks, and was able to take on a 'proficient' and increasingly 'expert role'.

M's evaluation shows that the predominant outcomes for him were in relation to his own development (the development of human capital), although he noted that 'the group bonded together, all the group participated on several if not all aspects of the project and shared ideas'.

In relation to Putnam's (2000) categories, M, like N, was also involved with work doing 'for'. He was a young white worker who did not live locally and who also had fewer existing skills relevant to the research project. He, like N, had quite high levels of association but mainly at inter-organization and group level rather than within the community. Like N, although generating social capital, his aim was to develop his human capital so that he could be involved in developing social capital in other settings.

B was a 'competent' team member and participated in team planning. Like M, B was not a community member and was a young white male. He did not therefore have access to much local knowledge, but had established a good working relationship with groups within the area, although he did not have a long term commitment to the community, and was very much undertaking the work 'for' the community.

He needed little support in relation to his levels of ability and had the potential to develop his skills and competence. He did, however, depend on community members of the team for networking and local resource information. He, therefore, had low levels of community association and only marginally higher levels of group and inter-organizational association due to his novice involvement in the area. In relation to the development of volunteers along the Dreyfus and Dreyfus (1980) spectrum he commented: 'In terms of experience then the worker has to be the "expert", however the group have developed expertise of their own'.

The outcomes for B also seem focused on his individual benefits, that is the human as opposed to the social capital elements, particularly in relation to the development of his work and his career, illustrated by his comments that 'I would like to continue to study community work at Masters level'.

Team member R had a short-lived involvement with the research, leaving partway into the fieldwork. Although he was a community member, had local knowledge and language skills, and despite trying to see if it was possible to link the project with his existing studies, he proved a marginal member of the team. He could be classed as a 'novice' as he needed intensive support, having not undertaken several elements of the research project training. However, he had high levels of association in the community at an agency level, high levels of local expertise and was involved in developing social capital. He prioritized these areas over the state capital elements of the project; that is, he concentrated his time on working for the community as opposed to that of the university project. He could be placed at the community activist end of the framework and ironically he may have been making the biggest contribution to social capital and civil renewal by deciding not to engage in our project team.

Team members F and Z were 'advanced beginners'; they had no experience of the type of approach we were using, but they were involved from the start of the project. They could, however, be classed as being expert within their own areas of community intervention, since they both possessed skills in community networking, local knowledge and community languages. They had high levels of association at a community and group level, although limited association at an inter-organization level. Both could be classed as active citizens.

F quickly moved on to become 'competent' and undertook large elements of the fieldwork on her own with minimal support, no doubt helped by her local knowledge and confidence in community settings. As a community member undertaking the project 'with' her community, F appears to have undertaken the work for social as well as her own individual capital. Both she and Z were definitely undertaking the work 'with' the community.

Z, although lacking in confidence, developed his research and interpersonal skills to the extent that he became 'competent' enough to undertake the organization of a large community event. He undertook a large part of the field research interviewing members of community groups and helped facilitate a team share day event. Like F, he was very definitely an expert within his geographical area and his expertise was drawn on by the rest of the team in relation to contacts and appropriate interventions.

Z, who had the lowest levels of expertise in relation to the technical research process, had one of the highest levels of local expertise. He also appears to have been aware of and developed the highest levels of social capital through his involvement. His own development in relation to confidence, skills and awareness were immense; however his emphasis in his evaluation was that of the benefit to local groups and the community. Although involved directly in the project for the University and so state capital, his priority was to the community and social capital benefits.

Interestingly, in their written accounts of their involvement in the research both Z and F predominantly used the term 'we' whereas other volunteers, particularly B and M who were working 'for' the community, talked from their own perspective, using 'I'. The differences within the team in relation to position could be seen to fit into the distinctions that Putnam (2000) calls 'doing for' and 'doing with'. The three white participants were all carrying out work in an altruistic way, 'doing for' the community, whereas the volunteers of Asian origin were carrying out the research for the benefit of the local communities (building social capital) and 'doing with' their communities, as well as individual benefit for themselves through the accredited training (human capital).

Each of the participants discussed in the case study undertook this process in differing ways, coming from a different starting point, based on their own experience and histories. The changes that took place were therefore different for each of the participants, and their requirements and contributions to the group process and outcomes also varied depending on their unique positions. The processes therefore differ depending on where the volunteer may be located on the volunteers' type framework (Table 4.2), particularly where they may be placed on a spectrum of novice to expert, cross cut with a 'doing with' and 'doing for' axis. The discussion here has shown that differing types and extents of change can be achieved at an individual (human) and community (social) level as a result of the process of discussion and experiential learning.

Who volunteers?

As can be seen from the analysis of the Tameside volunteers, each person had a different experience of the volunteering process. This was not only dependant on their skills, knowledge and confidence but also on who they were, their relationship to the community, and the activity. If voluntary activity is to be an empowering educational process it is important that we are aware of who is involved and who is excluded and why.

The history of youth and community work (see Davies, 1999) shows its origins as a philanthropy based activity of the white middle classes, coupled with self help activities of women and working people's groups. Volunteering has continued to attract people from different sections of the community and is difficult to quantify as demonstrated by the different types and definitions of volunteer discussed here.

It is also difficult to gauge the 'natural' level of community engagement as many people have become involved in volunteering as a result of government schemes, and most of the statistical indictors of volunteering represents those involved in formal volunteering programmes (as identified in the first category of volunteer type in Table 4.2). In 2005 government sources stated that there were 1.5 million more people involved in formal or informal voluntary activity than there were in 2001. This means that approximately 20 million people 'give up their free time to work for the benefit of others' (ODPM, 2005, p.9). However, there had been a decrease in membership of some groups such as women's organizations and an increase in membership of others, for example environmental groups. However, some authors such as Putnam (2000) and Field (2003) have suggested that volunteering continues to be carried out predominantly by the middle class, financially able, and quite often post retirement groups. From a review of studies of association in organizations and activities, Field concluded that 'volunteering and trust appear to be characteristics of the highly qualified and the middle class' (2003, p.75).

Statistics regarding the composition of who volunteers was gained for the production of the report of the Russell Commission (2005) and its successor the Youth Matters Green Paper (Department for Education and Skills, 2005). The reports recognized the value of volunteering, particularly for young people primarily in relation to developing their employability and thus human capital, but also to enable engagement in broader civic and civil participation (contributing to the development of social and state capital). Both documents recognized the potential exclusion of some young people from voluntary activities, and that action had to be taken to empower all citizens, primarily in relation to enabling them to work with public bodies to achieve common goals.

The three essential elements they identified to achieve this were, firstly, active citizenship; secondly, 'strengthened communities: community groups with the capacity and resources to bring people together to work out shared solutions' (HO 2005, p.7); and thirdly, partnership between public bodies and local people (Home Office Civil Renewal Unit, 'Together We Can' (2005).

Chapters 6 and 7 discuss how to enable participation and inclusive and representative practice. They discuss how to bring about involvement in these activities and raise debates over issues such as who benefits from voluntary involvement.

ACTIVITY 4.4

Analysing your group of volunteers in relation to levels of association and benefit

Having read the case study it will now be possible to analyse the involvement of your group of volunteers to help you recognize the complexity of their involvement and what may be the benefits for themselves the group, community and wider society, and their varying contributions to types of capital, social, human and state.

Task 4 levels of individual community involvement

'Volunteer'	Role e.g. volunteer, voluntary assistance, active citizen, self help, community activist	With or for	Association	Benefit	Capital
Example: CP	Active citizen	With	High	Community/individual	Social/human
Volunteer 1					
Volunteer 2					
Volunteer 3					
Volunteer 4					
Volunteer 5					

Conclusion

This chapter has used historical and theoretical perspectives to show the complexity and variety of types of volunteer, the roles they may undertake and their involvement within communities. The different outcomes and benefits have been discussed, making the case that some activities may be more for the benefit of the individual, whilst others may be more for community or government benefit, generating human, social or state capital. This was illustrated through analysis of the Tameside volunteer team.

The discussion has highlighted the benefits for the community of those involved 'with' as opposed to 'for' the community, and as a result has shown the differing requirements for volunteers. The volunteer type framework discussed here, which identifies types of benefit and the resulting capital, shows that the differing types of volunteers will have different implications for the Youth and Community Worker, whose role is to facilitate their effective involvement. The role of the worker in relation to volunteers is discussed in detail in the following chapter.

REFERENCES

Davies, B (1999) *A history of the youth service in England.* Leicester: Youth Work Press.

Department of Communities and Local Government (DLGC) (2006a) *The Community development challenge.* West Yorkshire: Communities and Local Government Publications.

Department of Communities and Local Government (DLGC) (2006b) *Citizenship survey 2005.* West Yorkshire: Communities and Local Government Publications.

Department for Education and Skills (2005) *Youth matters, Green Paper, consultation document.* London: HMSO, DFES.

Dewey, J (1916) *Democracy and education: An introduction to the philosophy of freedom.* New York: Free Press.

Dreyfus, H and Dreyfus, S (1980) A five stage model of the mental activities involved in directed skill acquisition. Unpublished report by the Air Force Office of Scientific Research [AFSC], USAF [contract F49620-79-0063], University of California, Berkeley.

Etzioni, A (1995) *The spirit of community: The reinvention of American society.* New York: Touchstone.

Etzioni, A (1997) *The new golden rule: Community and morality in a democratic society.* New York: Basic Books.

Field, J (2003) *Social capital.* London: Routledge.

Freire, P (1972) *Pedagogy of the oppressed.* London: Penguin Books.

Harris, K (2004) *Looking out for each other: The Manchester neighbourliness review.* Community Development Foundation.

Harris, K (2006) *Respect in the neighbourhood.* Dorset: Russell House Publishing.

Hodgson, L (2004) Manufactured civil society: Counting the cost: *Critical Social Policy* 79, Vol 24 (2) 139–164. London: Sage.

Home Office (2005) *Together we can.* London: Civil Renewal Unit, Home Office, TSO.

Office of the Deputy Prime Minister (ODPM) (2005) *Citizen engagement and public services: Why neighbourhoods matter.* London: ODPM.

Packham, C. et al. (2004) *Delivering effective volunteering.* Manchester: Manchester Metropolitan University, Community Audit and Evaluation Centre.

Packham, C. (2006) Doing us out of a job? Thesis for final completion of the Doctor of Education. Manchester: Manchester Metropolitan University.

Popple, K (2000) *Analysing community work. Its theory and practice.* Buckingham: Open University Press.

Prochaska, F (2002) *Schools of citizenship*: Charity and civic virtue. London: Civitas.

Putnam, RD (2000) *Bowling alone: The collapse and revival of American community*. New York: Simon and Schuster.

Russell Commission (2005) *Report: A national framework for youth action and engagement*. Russell Commission. London: HMSO.

Storrie, T (2004) *Citizens or what?*, in J Roche, ed., *Youth in society*. London: Sage, pp.52–60.

Taylor, AJP (1965) *English history, 1914–1945.* Oxford: Clarendon Press.

United Nations (2001) United Nations volunteers report, prepared for the UN General Assembly Special Session on Social Development. Geneva: UNO.

Chapter 5

The role of the Youth and Community Worker in relation to volunteers

This chapter discusses and clarifies the role of Youth and Community Workers in relation to volunteers, particularly in relation to government social policy which emphasizes community leadership and active citizenship. The volunteer type framework introduced in Chapter 3 is used to distinguish the differing roles for the worker in relation to the varying skills, knowledge and support needs of volunteers, active citizens and community activists. Examples are given from Barcelona and Tameside. The case is made that the relationship of workers to different types of volunteers is not purely based on their skills and knowledge, but that the worker has a role as an informal educator with whoever they work, be it service user, worker or volunteer, if the work being undertaken is to have the capacity to bring about change and social capital.

The context

Many professional Youth and Community Workers have become so following quite often long periods as volunteers, and have then undertaken professional training. As pointed out in 'The Community Development Challenge' (DCLG, 2006), 'entry to the (community development) profession has always included a special route via community activity. This is a distinctive feature of community development which is not available in other professions' (2006, p.34).

The role of the professional Youth and Community Worker is unusual in that it aims to foster rather than replace volunteers, who in some professions may be viewed as unqualified novices or amateurs. Voluntary, self help activity has always taken place, and in most cases without the support of Youth and Community Workers. In many countries such workers do not exist. In the United Kingdom, the role of Youth and Community Workers has been affected by the relationship of the community and voluntary sector to the state. When the state became involved in universal welfare provision after the Second World War in 1945, there was a reduction in the need for voluntary youth and community organizations and volunteers (Davies, 1999). Likewise Youth and Community Workers can be viewed to be filling gaps in provision and care not being provided by the state, by families or by communities. In societies and cultures where extended families and communities provide support and undertake self help activities there may never be a need for professional Youth and Community Work intervention.

Table 5.1 shows the development of Youth and Community Work in relation to volunteers and voluntary activity, outlining the relationship to that of the state and the provision of services by the state.

As the table reveals, there has been increased government emphasis on community engagement, particularly of volunteers and active citizens, and ways that may support the state rather than civil and community activity (this is discussed in Chapter 3). Before the establishment of such organizations as the Charity Organization Society (1869) (which supported the work of a range of organizations) there was little in the way of organizations that supported voluntary activity. From the 1860s onwards organizations supporting voluntary activity have developed to the extent that the Labour government in the United Kingdom now sees these organizations as a way of providing services that have previously been provided by the state, often through the involvement of volunteers.

The development of government interest in voluntary organizations and individuals is evident in the local government White Paper 'Strong and Prosperous Communities', which sets out a new agenda giving more power to local authorities and an improved relationship between 'local government and citizens' (DCLG, 2006, p.5). It identifies the need for support for citizens undertaking active citizenship type opportunities by saying that 'many citizens and community groups will need support to make the fullest use of them' (ibid.). These are particularly in relation to community capacity building, increasing skills and confidence to engage.

As discussed in Chapter 2 on informal education, the aim of Youth and Community Work is to facilitate and enable self help and activity which has been freely chosen. It is therefore to be expected that much of their work will be with volunteers and those involved in self help activities. The government initiatives cited above, which have promoted volunteers, active citizenship and community leaders, have made it essential for Youth and Community Workers to clarify and redefine their role.

There is the potential for Youth and Community Workers to have a role in facilitating and supporting such initiatives, and to see the emphasis on community involvement and voice as empowering. However, we also have to evaluating critically these social policy initiatives and the intended role of voluntary activity. As discussed in relation to civil and civic involvement (in Chapter 3) we must ask whether these initiatives are a means to get active citizens to do work that was previously done by the state, such as community guardians to police neighbourhoods, volunteers to replace welfare services, community leaders to 'Do us out of a job' (Packham et al., 2006) and make Youth and Community Workers redundant.

This might not be a bad thing if the loss of Youth and Community Workers was a sign of vibrant and self supporting communities. Currently the emphasis on community cohesion, safety, surveillance and the privatization of welfare services would indicate that the purpose of such moves are less about empowerment than self policing and social control, often targeted at the most excluded communities. It is therefore likely, though not essential, that we shall need to continue our role of facilitating the independence of community and volunteering activity, and to enable it to be an educational and transformational activity.

This chapter explores the complexity of the volunteer/worker relationship, and the need for an informal education approach to volunteer involvement.

Table 5.1 Volunteering and Youth and Community Work in relation to government policy

Volunteer role	State role	Role of Youth and Community Work professional
Self help and philanthropic.		
Charity Organization Society (1869).	Juvenile Organization Committees (1916).	
	Local Youth Committees (1939).	
	The Challenge of Youth (1940), state to support the work of voluntary organizations.	
	Large scale intervention in welfare (1945).	Reduction in role of youth and community organizations. Workers and organizations supplement the role of the state.
Reduced role, emphasis on professionals.	Albemarle Report, increase in role of state in youth sector (1960).	Establishment of full and part-time training courses for workers. Shift of emphasis to full-time professional workers.
Revert to philanthropic and benevolent role.	Conservative government (1979) reduction in services, and role of state. Emphasis on private and voluntary sector, and support to volunteering.	Increase in role of community and voluntary sector.
	Rejection of Thompson Report (1982) and its call for states role in youth provision. Government support of volunteering schemes e.g. Princes Trust.	Dissatisfaction with role and call for a radical/critical approach, e.g. Smith, Creators not Consumers, 1982.
Volunteering for: • human capital; • community cohesion (social capital); • surveillance; • control; • civic engagement (state capital, generative and punitive). Volunteering becomes compulsory!	New Labour and the Third Way (1997–). State intervention in the third sector. Increased role of private and voluntary sector in the work of the state. Reduction in state support for Youth and Community sector. Increase in targeted work. Creation of 'active citizens'.	Facilitation and empowering role. Active citizens' potential to challenge role of professional workers. Need to clarify and re-establish role: • as informal, social and political educators; • able to provide varied role for different volunteers; • able to critique and challenge state capital.

ACTIVITY **5.1**

Helping volunteer involvement

Considering a situation in which you were a volunteer (of any of the types discussed in Chapter 3), please list at least five factors that helped your participation and effective involvement and five that may have hindered this.

Insert the volunteer activity in the left hand column and the factors that may have helped or hindered your involvement in the other columns. For example, in the left hand column you might have been involved as a volunteer in a school walking bus scheme, which was helped because your child went to the school so you knew the parents and children. However, it might have been hindered as you did not live in the area and did not know good routes for walking, etc.

Type of volunteer role	Factors that helped your role/involvement	Factors that hindered your role/involvement

Considering what you have recorded in the table, you will have started to identify what the requirements are to enable you and other people to work effectively as and with volunteers.

Butcher (2003), when discussing organizational practice for what Banks, Butcher and Robertson term 'community practice', also identifies different categories and roles of active citizens which he suggests will influence the type of organizational and worker relationship. These are:

- **active citizen as consumer** – active in pursuing their rights to services, as users and clients;

- **citizens as governors** – what he terms owner-authorizers, for example people involved in neighbourhood councils, and as voters;

- **doers** – self helpers who are active in producing 'public value for themselves and other citizens'. (Butcher, 2003, p.69)

Similarly, the different types of volunteers and their support requirements have been recognized by Charles Woodd, the then Implementation Manager for the Civil Renewal Unit in the Home Office (Woodd, 2005). He identified four related areas of citizen or voluntary involvement: the citizen governor, activist, managed volunteer in a voluntary organization, and member/volunteer in a community group. He recommended that 'development support, for example through information, training and community development, will need to be tailored to each citizen role. Good practice information, advice and technical services are needed to enable citizens in such roles to interact effectively with the organization and agencies around them to be able to bring about positive change' (Woodd, 2005, np).

Support requirements for different volunteers

As identified in Chapter 3 and discussed above, there are many different ways that volunteers are involved in a range of activities. It could be suggested that those volunteers who are inexperienced will require more support and supervision. This is shown in the adaptation of the Dreyfus and Dreyfus (1980) framework below.

Table 5.2 Support requirements for categories of volunteers, amended from Table 5.1 and adapted from Dreyfus and Dreyfus (1980)

Support requirements by Youth and Community Worker	Category of volunteer
Intensive support	Novice, an unskilled/inexperienced volunteer
Medium support	Advanced beginner, possessing some skill and knowledge in limited areas
Minimal support	Competent, more skilled, able to plan consciously, application of longer term goals
Partnership	Proficient, quickly able to act as effective co-worker, showing sensitivity and skill
Reciprocal 'support', and induction	Expert, high levels of proficiency, both skills and knowledge of value to the agency

The Dreyfus and Dreyfus framework is very task specific and does not recognize other skills and knowledge that community members may possess and which may be invaluable to the task to be undertaken, for example, language skills, awareness of where people meet, their interests, appropriate methods. Experts should therefore be redefined as those who meet the requirements of skills and knowledge that are needed to undertake the work to be carried out with high levels of proficiency of value to the agency or activity. This implies that the idea of expert can be context specific and that more importantly it can be locally defined, for example, if someone has an understanding of the norms and requirements of an agency or their own community. This is illustrated in the following case study.

CASE STUDY

The workers at the La Verneda project in Barcelona, a self help, community based adult education project working on Freirian principles, received many offers of volunteer input from trained teachers. However, although these volunteers possessed high levels of skill and knowledge about their subject area, their lack of understanding and familiarity with the approach and methods of the La Verneda centre meant that they were novices in relation to the specific ethos and norms of the project. This required a high degree of supervision and longer periods of induction than volunteers who had been part of the centre programmes, and so were familiar with their underlying ethos and approach, but who may have possessed fewer skills.

The Dreyfus and Dreyfus (1980) model therefore proved simplistic and highly functional in relation to the volunteers within this project as it did not include the element of existing knowledge and shared value base or ideology.

Youth and Community Workers working with different types of volunteers therefore have to be aware of the different types of voluntary involvement, and the complexity of the relationship between the worker and the volunteer. We may work with volunteers as groups, such as community forums, where our role may be to support their activities, share information and facilitate the involvement of under-represented interests on the forum. We will also work with individual volunteers, where our role will be to help them determine what is the best use of their skills and knowledge both for their own development and that of the group or community. In all cases our role is still that of informal educator to involve volunteers in the process of community learning as discussed in Chapter 2

Volunteers and informal education

The worker/volunteer relationship is complex. Not only are the levels of proficiency identified above context specific, but even if the volunteer could be deemed expert they should still be involved in informal education processes. For example, a new volunteer in a small voluntary organization, who is an excellent IT specialist, may hold homophobic views and may have been overheard making derogatory jokes. They may not require induction in relation to the technical task, but they should be involved in a process of discussion of the norms of the project and made aware of the way their comments are reinforcing negative stereotypes and perpetuating exclusion of some project members. This can be done informally, formally through supervision or through debate at team meetings. Informal education should not solely take place with volunteers, service users and participants in our activities. We should apply the same principles and methods when we are carrying out training and supporting workers.

Following the characteristics of informal education outlined in Chapter 2, Youth and Community Workers should facilitate the participation of community members, of which volunteering is an example. This might be encouraging people to take part in committees and democratic structures, or as a part of self help groups that are taking action on local issues. This horizontal and vertical participation is discussed in detail in Chapter 6 on enabling participation. They can be encouraged to participate but also to analyse and evaluate the activity they may already be involved in and how it can be made more effective, for example, by making alliances with other groups involved in similar activities at a local or national level.

Activity is an essential element of Youth and Community Work. It is the basis for experiential learning and reflection, through dialogue and praxis. Facilitated learning that reflects on voluntary activity is central to the Take Part Active Learning for Active Citizenship programmes. The voluntary activity, or group action, is the basis for learning and discussion through the informal education process. This is illustrated by the examples of Schools of Participation outlined in Chapter 8, which discusses the facilitation of community learning.

A further essential element of the informal education process in relation to voluntary involvement is to ensure that we counter exclusion and consider the factors that may prevent people from volunteering or from being under-represented in relation to volunteer activity of any type. This is discussed in Chapter 4 on who volunteers. Putting strategies in place to involve community members who are excluded is increasingly viewed as essential for effective and cohesive communities. This is obviously for the benefit of the potential volunteer. In addition associational activities and volunteering are recognized as being important contributors to the generation of community bonds (Etzioni, 1995, 1997) and social capital (Putnam, 2000).

However, exclusion from some types of engagement is not confined to disadvantaged groups. European studies have shown that 'those who have the highest levels of social (and human) capital are the most selective when it comes to political participation' and increasingly their involvement in volunteering also stems from 'a desire for self realization' (Field, 2003, p.98) rather than philanthropy.

In relation to volunteering schemes with young people, the report of the Russell Commission (2005) and its successor the 'Youth Matters' Green Paper (Department for Education and Skills, 2005) recognized that there were particular groups who were under-represented as volunteers (for example disabled young people and young people from black and ethnic minority communities). The reports identified general as well as specific barriers to participation, and strategies for overcoming these were suggested, for example, induce-ments such as accreditation, and practical assistance such as payments of expenses, as well as ensuring a range of appropriate and flexible volunteering opportunities. Youth and Community Workers should therefore look at ways of enabling self help and voluntary activity for all groups and communities and removing specific as well as general barriers to involvement, as will be discussed below.

Informal education with a team of volunteers

My facilitation of the team outlined in Chapter 4 is used here to illustrate the use of informal education with volunteers. The focus of the work was to identify the requirements for effective volunteering for those involved with community and voluntary groups in Tameside (a metropolitan area to the east of Manchester). The work with the team was carried out to facilitate group discussion and negotiation, rather than to direct a set curriculum. Sessions started from the experience, concerns and strengths of the participants. Issues were discussed, tasks and problems identified (the process of what Freire calls problem posing) and strategies agreed. I was aware that I was an external facilitator, 'doing for' the group (Putnam, 2000), and although I possessed valuable skills and experience these were primarily related to abstract knowledge and general skills. I was technically an expert, as I was a professionally qualified worker and was delivering the training to be undertaken to support the participatory community audit. As members of local community groups the volunteers were expert within their own community in relation to knowledge, networking, effective communication and in understanding local requirements. The dialogue with the team enabled them to share their context specific knowledge so that appropriate methods could be devised and action agreed. Issues of power, inclusion and difference were central to our debates to enable the research to be inclusive. This included discussions of the roles of the various key stakeholders in the area, identifying gate keepers, and blocks and barriers to participation. My role was to enable a space for critical dialogue to reflect on and plan the participatory research, and to enable a process of transformation and change to take place. The team findings were shared with members of community and voluntary groups in Tameside, and they jointly wrote the final report, which has been used to inform local practice and that of the Manchester Metropolitan University's volunteering programme, coMMUni.

The findings from their work are also used below as a basis for the requirements for effective volunteering.

The process of active learning, enabling reflection on the action that was taking place, was an essential element of the informal education process with the team of volunteers. As a result each of them was becoming a more active citizen, within the research team and within their own communities. One of the participants gained such high levels of confidence and expertise that he progressed from being a football coach to organizing the Mela community festival in Tameside!

As I have discussed in Chapter 3, some of the participants were more able than others to undertake this process. Each came with a different starting point based on their own experience and histories. If I had taken on a directive 'expert' role as opposed to a facilitating and enabling one, the opportunities for skill and knowledge sharing and development would have been lost, with consequent reduction in the value, applicability, and reliability of the outcomes for all concerned.

Freire discussed this process of sharing between the worker and 'learner' and stated 'the problem-posing educator constantly reforms (his) reflections in the reflections of the students, the students are now critical co-investigators in dialogue with the teacher' (Freire, 1972, p.54), including the essential role of critical reflection for both worker and participant. This approach is similar to what Walker called being a 'subaltern professional' (1996), describing the professional working alongside people, not for them. By doing this I am in the process of developing 'organic intellectuals' (Walker, 1996). With the Tameside volunteers this meant that all decisions about the design, content, analysis and report production of the community audit research was negotiated and carried out by the whole team, for example the questions to be asked, the plan and methods to be used, the data analysis, and report writing. This co-learning process necessitates a commitment to praxis, the ongoing cyclical process of action and reflection: 'critical reflection on our conditioning by our cultural context, on our way of acting, and on our values is indispensable' (Freire, 1992, p.79).

It is therefore essential that the workers' role verifies the participants' experience and, as facilitator, enables the team to generate and own their own knowledge and actions. The dilemma for the Youth and Community Worker is to be aware of their own power and position in relation to those that they work with and those that they work for, and to judge if their involvement is generating state as well as individual and social capital, contributing to civil and civic engagement (these debates are discussed further in Chapter 3).

Organizational implications for the role of the professional Youth and Community Worker

It is not only important to understand the different types of volunteers and their possible requirements, and to involve all in informal education processes. It is also important to recognize the organizational implications for effective support for volunteers of all types.

The research (Packham et al., 2004) carried out by the Tameside volunteer team, with members from 26 voluntary organizations, aimed to identify the requirements for effective volunteer involvement. The findings showed that encouragement from workers and professional development opportunities were rated more highly than financial considerations. Volunteers indicated the importance of being supported by a professional worker and being given positive feedback and the identification of action points. The volunteers felt that their own and the workers' roles should be equally valued, and that they should have mutual respect, work for common goals, and share skills and information. This supports the requirement for a co-worker approach as discussed above (Freire, 1972 and Walker, 1996). The research also showed that most of the volunteers, although feeling they had skills and knowledge to offer, were involved in administrative type activities. This indicates that workers may be undervaluing the existing knowledge and skills that the volunteers possess and bring to an activity or organization. Volunteers also cited the barriers to volunteering as being agency related, ranging from a lack of appreciation of the role of volunteers, to lack of time, structure and training, as well as a lack of financial support, and linguistic and cultural barriers. Whereas volunteers' own requirements were important factors, twice as many responses indicated perceived or actual organizational issues as being important deterrents equally as restricting as practical issues for volunteers.

These findings indicated that Youth and Community Workers and organizations need to have the capacity to engage with volunteers, and that they must consider the factors that may act as barriers to volunteering. Additionally the research indicated that there was often a view from workers that volunteers were all novices, not recognizing and utilizing the actual or potential capacity that they possessed.

Although recognizing that the worker has a skilled role in facilitating volunteer involvement, particularly in the case of those who may be 'doing for' and have little context specific knowledge, the 'expertise' of volunteers and active citizens must be recognized. The findings also indicate the requirement for co-operative and co-investigational working, including the essential role of critical reflection, a problem posing approach where the worker and volunteers act together on tasks (Freire,1972).

From the research findings it is therefore possible to draw up a list of possible barriers to volunteer involvement that need to be acted upon by Youth and Community Workers. The table below shows some types of barriers and illustrates how they may be apparent.

Table 5.3 Possible institutional and organizational barriers to volunteering

Possible barrier	Illustration of barrier
Lack of training	Requirements for particular skills or knowledge that the volunteer may not have
Lack of induction into organization, task or role	Complex organizational policies and procedures Unclear roles and responsibilities Lack of familiarity with the work of the agency
Lack of information	About the organization, aims, vision and ongoing activities
Lack of communication	Being excluded from decision making or planning
Lack of appreciation of role of volunteer	Being given a role that does not utilize the volunteer's skills, knowledge and abilities
Lack of structure	Tasks and time scales not being negotiated, or clear Accountability unclear Team membership unclear
Lack of financial support	Failure to reimburse for travel, materials, meals and child care costs
Access/exclusion	Physical, practical, and 'cultural' barriers such as lack of a crèche, norms that exclude groups and individuals (e.g. homophobic), lack of accessible venues, materials, inappropriate timing
Lack of awareness of linguistic and cultural barriers	Not providing materials in languages other than English, not meeting varied dietary and religious requirements (e.g. a prayer space), not having single sex work, activities that are alcohol based (e.g. held in a social centre, based around cheese and wine)
Need for regular supervision	Worker does not ensure that the above factors are acknowledged and overcome, and the volunteer given space to discuss their work and development

---

ACTIVITY 5.2

The above table identifies some of the factors that may hinder voluntary involvement. Combining this with the factors you have identified in the initial activity, those that may have hindered your involvement in a voluntary activity, now identify what could have been done to support your or another volunteer's involvement.

You could draw on the Take Part learning framework (www.takepart.org) and Occupational Standards for Volunteer Management to assist you (see also www.NCVO-vol.org.uk, and the National Occupational Standards for Managing Volunteers (NCVO, 2004) for more detail on organizational and structural requirements for effective working with volunteer).

Conclusion

In this chapter I have aimed to show that volunteers are an important asset to community groups and within communities. This has been recognized by many government social policy initiatives, which, as discussed in this book, see different types of volunteering activities as being valuable for personal development, community cohesion, service identification and delivery of community governance. It is therefore essential that we do not see volunteers as novices, but should recognize our role in relation to enabling their involvement to be effective, and as participants in communities and groups to be part of an empowering, self help, informal education, community learning processes.

However, applying informal education principles to work with volunteers requires that we are involved in a critical dialogue which may question the nature and role of volunteers and particularly some of the policies in relation to volunteering. For example, where voluntary activity is compulsory for some (e.g. school children and offenders) and impossible for others (e.g. asylum seekers, where volunteering may be deemed as unpaid 'work' which they are legally not allowed to undertake).

The requirement for Youth and Community Workers is that we should have both a functional and educational role in relation to volunteers. To do this we must

a) understand better the complex nature of the volunteer role;

b) appreciate the contributions made by volunteers;

c) be able to facilitate effective volunteering, of whatever type;

d) understand the organizational requirements of effective volunteering and implement them;

e) be prepared and able to provide opportunities for informal education with volunteers, so that their contributions are set in a broader community and societal context;

f) work to enable volunteering to be an empowering and self help process open to all;

g) think critically about social policy in relation to volunteering, and our role in supporting or challenging these initiatives.

Youth and Community Workers therefore have a clear role and expertise in relation to volunteer involvement. However, Youth and Community Workers have been reluctant to view themselves as experts and, as Thomas wrote, 'there is ambivalence in community work about the idea of expertise . . . the notion of "the expert" is contrary to the spirit of community work' (1983, p.185). The role of the worker is that we should empower those with whom we work, therefore challenging the usual powerful status of the expert. Thomas, however, goes on to argue that

> *the trained and paid community worker is or ought to have expertise in her work; without such expertise there is no justification for the training and salary such people receive, and no justification for the trust and responsibility given them by employers and groups. The fact that part of the worker's expertise is to pass on his skills and knowledge, and to do so participatively, is not to deny that workers' expertise; rather it indicates the need for expertise, not just in community organizing but in the role of the informal educator. (Thomas, 1983, p.185)*

The discussion and analysis in this chapter has highlighted the complexity of the work being undertaken. As a professional Youth and Community Worker I believe that key aspects of informal education should underpin our work, those of space for associational critical dialogue, voluntary engagement, the control and self direction of an active educational process, and lastly a critical perspective which takes into account issues of power and exclusion. In addition to these characteristics it is essential that we set Youth and Community Work in context, although much of what we do is for the short term benefit of those we work with, and primarily achieves human capital, our longer term aim should be to facilitate voluntary involvement that contributes to social capital and the benefit of wider civil and civic society. To be able to achieve this we need to be aware of the political consequences of our intervention, and the impact of undertaking work that may be primarily producing benefits for the state as opposed to the community.

REFERENCES

Butcher, H (2003) *Organizational management for community practice,* in S Banks, H Butcher, P Henderson, P and J Robertson, eds, *Managing community practice.* Bristol: Policy Press, pp.57–83.

Davies, B (1999) *A history of the youth service in England.* Leicester: Youth Work Press.

Department of Communities and Local Government (DGLG) (2006) *The community development challenge.* West Yorkshire: DCLG (www.communities.gov.uk).

Department of Communities and Local Government (DGLG) (2006) *Strong and prosperous communities.* London: DCLG.

Department for Education and Skills (DFES) (2005) *Youth matters, Green Paper, consultation document.* London: HMSO, DFES.

Dreyfus, H and Dreyfus, S (1980) A five stage model of the mental activities involved in directed skill acquisition. Unpublished report by the Air Force Office of Scientific Research [AFSC], USAF [contract F49620-79-0063], University of California, Berkeley.

Etzioni, A (1995) *The spirit of community: The reinvention of American society.* New York: Touchstone.

Etzioni, A (1997) *The new golden rule: Community and morality in a democratic society.* New York: Basic Books.

Field, J (2003) *Social capital.* London: Routledge.

Freire, P (1972) *Pedagogy of the oppressed.* London: Penguin Books.

Freire, P (1992) *Pedagogy of hope.* New York: Continuum.

Packham, C. et al. (2004) *Delivering effective volunteering*. Manchester: Manchester Metropolitan University, Community Audit and Evaluation Centre.

Packham, C. (2006) Doing us out of a job? Thesis for final completion of the Doctor of Education. Manchester: Manchester Metropolitan University.

Putnam, RD (2000) *Bowling alone: The collapse and revival of American community*. New York: Simon and Schuster.

Russell Commission (October 2004) *The Russell Commission on youth action and engagement, consultation document*, London: HMSO.

Thomas, DN (1983) *The making of community work.* London: George Allen and Unwin.

Walker, M (1996) Subaltern professionals: Acting in the pursuit of social justice. *Educational Action Research*, 4 (3): pp.407–425.

Woodd, C (2005) Head of implementation team, Civil Renewal Unit, Home Office Email Communication with Carol Packham. July to September.

Chapter 6
Enabling participation in communities

This chapter draws on the discussion of informal education practice and civil and civic involvement, particularly in relation to individuals as volunteers, and considers ways that we can facilitate their participation. Different types and structures for participation are outlined to help you understand the complex nature of participation. You are asked to identify blocks and barriers at an individual and organizational level and strategies to enable participation are suggested.

The importance of participation

Enabling participation is a central aim of Youth and Community Work. Facilitating effective participation enables communities to have a voice and agency, and it assists service providers and policy makers to make sure that what they do is wanted and required, so being more efficient and effective.

As set out in Chapter 2, Enabling Informal Education, making space for active, discussion based participation to take place is a central element of the informal education process. Alongside this is a role for Youth and Community Workers to help participants have self determined and directed voluntary engagement that will bring about change. Workers should also facilitate inclusion by challenging the barriers to participation that community members may face. Ledwith states 'community work is about the active participation of people in their own transformation' (Ledwith, 1997, p.13).

This chapter shows the importance of participation for enabling community members to have influence and to bring about change. I identify the complexities of participation in relation to the different types of groups that community members may work with, and note how some groups provide greater opportunity for participation and influence than others.

Tasks are included to enable you to analyse the different types of groups participation and to suggest what you as a Youth and Community Worker can do to overcome barriers and enable increased levels of participation.

Participation enshrined in social policy

I write at a time when community members who were seen as volunteers and good neighbours are now being viewed by government programmes as active citizens, and where all citizens are being encouraged to have a voice in determining what is needed for their communities and how it should be delivered. In addition, participation, an essential element of the empowerment process for Youth and Community Workers, has become enshrined in government policy as an essential element of social inclusion and community engagement agendas. For example, the 'Duty to Involve' is a key element of the Local Government and Public Involvement in Health Act 2007 and represents a change in the way in which councils are expected to engage with local people in the design and delivery of services. From 2007 'there will be a duty for all best value authorities, including local authorities, to inform, consult and involve the people they serve' (DCLG, 2007).

With regard to young people, Article 12 of the UN Convention on the Rights of the Child (ratified in the UK in 1991) says 'all children and young people have a right to a say on all issues that affect them and for their views to be taken seriously'. This right to participation and to be heard has been further enshrined in the five outcomes of 'Every Child Matters', which sets out that every child from birth to 19 'should have the support they need to be healthy, stay safe, enjoy and achieve, make a positive contribution and achieve economic well-being' (Department of Health, 2004). For examples see www.participationworks.org.uk

---

ACTIVITY 6.1

Choose a situation in which young people or members of community groups have participated in an activity. Consider and record the benefits of their participation

Who is involved (the stakeholders in the activity)?	The benefits of participation
Community member/young person/service user	
Group, community or agency	
Sponsor, funder or lead department	
Wider society	
Government (policy, etc.), other national body?	

Your answers in the table should indicate that participation and initiatives to encourage participation are a positive opportunity to enable service users and community members to have a voice in the decisions that affect their lives and the directions that their communities will take. However, government interventions should be critiqued on the basis of 'for whose benefit' and whether the activities actually bring about meaningful change.

This chapter will develop your awareness of the different types of structures for participation and the barriers to participation and the role of the worker in relation to enabling participation.

Participation and active citizenship

As discussed in the introduction, the involvement of service users and community members is recognized as important for the well being of communities and their members. This involvement was previously viewed as being a good neighbour, or wider involvement as a volunteer seen as 'giving something back' or being an altruistic or self help activity. English government schemes have formalized these activities through volunteering programmes, garnering the expertise of the community and voluntary sector in the delivery of services and through attempts to encourage citizen engagement, or active citizenship.

As discussed in Chapter 3, on civic and civil engagement, it is important to evaluate whether the contribution that is being made by individual citizens and groups is for the benefit of the development of a vibrant community and civil society or for the benefit of the state, government policy makers and service providers, civic society. It is obviously possible to do both, but the dilemmas for workers who support these processes and for citizen participants is that the increased emphasis on civic engagement may reduce the amount of time, energy and resources to take part in community generated activities. The result of this is that it may reduce the potential to create social movements and bring about radical change.

A Champions of Participation conference in 2007 brought together representatives from (all working in local government) 15 countries to explore 'the problems and potential for strengthening citizen participation in local government' (Dunn et al., 2007, p.2). The report concluded that

> *participation is at the heart of democracy, it is not just a means of delivering government targets, or driving service improvements. Around the world, participation is recognized as a means of tackling poverty, inequality, and discrimination, empowering citizens, building strong communities and achieving social change. The bigger vision of 'democratizing everyday life' should be at the centre of the government's approach. (Dunn et al., 2007, p.37)*

The theme of this book is how we engage with community members, and what our role is as Youth and Community Workers. This text makes the case that we have a role as an informal educator with whomsoever we work, recognizing that some people and groups may require more facilitation or support than others, and at different times of their lives.

Informal education processes in community activities

Arnstein's (1969) ladder of participation, which has eight types of participation, is often cited as a spectrum to indicate characteristics or degrees of community involvement ranging from community manipulation to citizen control and self determination. At one end of the ladder, there is virtually no self directed participation by community members; at the other, activity is fully controlled and directed by them. The ladder is also used to show the relationship between Youth and Community Workers and community members, implying that there is a high level of worker control in the manipulation level and no need for worker involvement where citizens have control. Most Youth and Community Work is assumed to take place in the mid-range of activities where there is partnership between the community and worker. However, there is a role for the worker as informal educator at all stages of the ladder, to enable participation to be most effective. For example, where there are high levels of participation the worker can act as ally and support community activity. At all points on the ladder individuals and groups can be involved in informal education processes that enable the making of space for deliberation, work towards self direction and inclusive practices, and enable transformation and change. Even in situations where participants do not feel they have much power, acting as a group can enable people to be more aware of the issues involved and can take part in an analysis of what is possible at an individual, cultural and global level (see Thompson, 2001, and the PCS model discussed in Chapter 7).

Enabling participation

We are all part of many groups and different communities. These may be based on geography or neighbourhood or with people that we share interests or identity. Some of these groups will have come about naturally, such as peer groups and families; others will have come together for particular purposes and may be focused on tasks. It is likely that a community or self formed group will have higher levels of participation and commitment than one formed 'externally' or where participation is enforced (for example, schools).

It is important that we recognize the different types of groups, how activity takes place in groups, and the ways that people may be involved or excluded in order to help us effectively enable participation within groups and community activities.

Types of groups and group life

Tuckman and Jensen (1977) identified that all groups, whether formed or natural, self deter-mined or enforced, went though similar patterns of group life. These were identified as:

- **forming**, when the participants are coming together, even if they know each other they may be involved in a new task;

- **storming**, where debate and argument will be at its height when agreeing what is to be done and how, who by etc.;

- **norming**, when agreement has been reached;

- **performing**, when the task of the group is being carried out;

- **adjourning**, when the task is complete and the group may cease or make plans to evaluate and move on to other activities.

As indicated in Chapter 3, on informal education, the role of the worker is to enable people to take part in groups, where they help create spaces for critical dialogue and debate. Here participants may be supported to undertake self directed, inclusive and empowering activities that bring about change.

A facilitator of a group can therefore act as a

- visionary: sharing a vision of what can be achieved, particularly in the early stages of any activity;

- motivator: inspiring people to get involved in the forming stage, and to stay involved in the later stages of a group; or

- catalyst: enabling people to discover what it is they want to explore and to help them decide what they might need for that exploration. (adapted from the Take Part learning framework, DCLG, 2006, p.67)

In the same way that workers may have differing roles depending on the stage of the group's life, they may also have differing roles in relation to the 'formality' of the situation. For example, it is possible to be involved in a learning process in an unplanned way in a spontaneous, natural group having the same aims and principles. Alternatively, learning can take place through a planned or formed activity such as a 'constructed conversation', or a programme designed to result in action, as in the example of the Schools of Participation. Both are illustrated here.

Constructed conversations

Constructed conversations work from the principle that citizens have the potential competence to identify issues and injustices in their communities. However, for this to happen efficiently, citizens need support. These conversations are mostly informal but have a structure and are enabled by a facilitator who operates as a 'critical and constructive friend' to help people:

- establish and build relationships with people with whom they would not normally connect;

- explore themes as they arise in the dialogue – participants have the freedom to develop the conversational topics as a collaborative process;

- develop self awareness and the confidence to engage with people and organizations;

- see connections between observation and action – recognize links between actions and consequences;

- look beyond themselves and their own issues; and

- produce not only expected but also unexpected outcomes, which work towards strengthening the community at large.

This approach recognizes the need for individuals and groups to act as catalysts to support self organizing and self constructed communities which contribute to the further development of civil society. These are referred to as 'self organizing processes', which can be understood as how people go about making relationships, working together, organizing, and working in groups and as individuals to develop civil society.

> **CASE STUDY**
>
> **Constructed conversations on the theme of migrant workers' rights**
>
> *The Lincoln ALAC hub supported a space for informal learning for adults recently arrived in the UK looking for work and also for those providing employment and services to this new workforce.*
>
> *From the perspective of citizenship, those arriving in the UK have a complex identity: legal seasonal and migrant workers are eligible to vote in local elections provided a period of residency can be proved, but there are barriers to creating such a democratic identity – including challenges in accessing accommodation, dealing with financial services, inter-pretation, and in connecting with the UK establishment. Beyond legal eligibility, there are gaps in community education about rights and responsibilities, within both new and established communities, which can be addressed in whole or in part by structured informal learning processes.*
>
> *If people are to become active citizens there is a need to tackle the wider issues of social exclusion through learning. Barriers to engagement need to be overcome, for example by connecting people and showing that participation can improve their experience of life in the UK. Issues of importance identified include:*
>
> - *housing and employment;*
> - *access to health and other services;*
> - *understanding English law;*
> - *relationships with the authorities/institutions;*
> - *relationships with indigenous communities.*
>
> *The ALAC group facilitators worked with groups of providers and migrant workers to increase their understanding of these issues and to help them get better at communicating their needs and engaging more actively in shaping their civil environments. This was a practical, sustained engagement focusing on providing participants with space to reflect and to reorganize themselves and their activities.*
>
> *(Zoraida Mendiwelso-Bendek Lincoln ALAC/Take Part hub and Chair of the National Take Part network)*

As the name implies, these 'facilitated' group learning processes are constructed or formed spaces. This method is also the basis for what are called Schools of Participation.

Schools of Participation

This is based on a Latin American model of community leadership training. The content of the facilitated groups process is approached through action learning where participants engage in an extended collective process where individual experiences are drawn upon and linked to theories and methodologies. This process facilitates the journey through the following elements and draws out links and relationships between them:

- the individuals' experience and context;

- the group and community;

- the wider regional and national structures;

- the global situation.

The final part of the group process allows participants to identify jointly a collective action that responds to the issues and learning identified during the 'School', or already agreed as a theme for the group. This can also be used to reflect on individual action as a volunteer or active citizen.

The process and content is shaped by the participants. Issues brought by the participants influence the types of power structures explored and analysed and the issues raised by participants influence the extended range of theories, skills, methods and tools covered in the group sessions. The approach is based on the Freirian (1972) popular education models discussed in Chapter 2, where individual participants are enabled to discuss critically their situations or issues by drawing on their experiences in order to pose a problem and subsequently analyse it, becoming more aware of the factors influencing them and the world, with a view to making transformational change.

CASE STUDY

A School of Participation for members of the Deaf community in Greater Manchester, January 2006–March 2007

Recruitment and setting up of the school
Community Pride has a Deaf Linkwork Project and a Deaf Linkworker and over a period of time has built up good contacts with a variety of Deaf groups in Greater Manchester, including Manchester Deaf Centre and the Salford Deaf Gathering. Over a period of months each group was visited and Deaf people were invited to participate in the School. It is always difficult to explain to people exactly what a School is, but it was particularly challenging to explain the concept in British Sign Language! We decided to begin by inviting people to come to some sessions to learn about how to make a video and then to think about how a video could be used as a tool for communication. This proved a valuable first step in recruiting people to the School. We managed to gather a group of about 12 people from five different parts of Greater Manchester and met fortnightly for about nine months. We had a mix of men and women and a reasonable age range.

Delivering the School
It was important for the Deaf community that the facilitator was a Deaf person and that the hearing people involved were clear about their supporting role. The Community Pride Linkworker acted as the facilitator with support from two hearing staff from Community Pride. As a School of Participation seeks to enable participants to address issues of power in

their communities, it was vital to confront the power imbalance between the hearing world and the Deaf Community at the very beginning. All the sessions were conducted through British Sign Language and interpreters worked with the hearing staff.

Many of the early sessions involved using a range of creative techniques to encourage the participants to identify current issues for Deaf people. There were many issues highlighted, including communication, transport, access to libraries, lack of Deaf awareness and barriers to employment. It took several sessions to work through the issues until it was felt that access to Job Centres and employment information was a major concern. The group agreed to do some research and members of the School undertook a 'mystery shopper' exercise going into various Job Centres asking for information. Their experiences were brought back to the group and analysed so that an action plan could be designed to bring about some kind of change.

Action for change

The group agreed that a short training video should be made accompanied by some case studies and training materials for Job Centre Plus Managers and staff. The video was written and made by the group with the support of Manchester Community Information Network. The group called the video 'Turning the world upside down' and it involved a clever reversal of roles. The video showed a hearing person going for a job where all the staff were Deaf and there were no interpreters! The video used British Sign Language and there was a voiceover for hearing people. A seminar was organized in November 2006 for the Department of Work and Pensions staff and others, and the video and training materials were launched.

Impact

Members of the group developed confidence and a range of new skills which have since been used for further work around other issues. The video and materials proved useful for the training of front-line staff at Job Centres and challenged unhelpful stereotypes of Deaf people. Rather than problematizing the Deaf community the School exposed the barriers to communication within the hearing world.

(Anne Stewart, Community Pride Initiative, 2008)

Most of the examples above could be classified as **horizontal** community engagements that contribute to civil society, generating what Putnam (2000) called social capital.

However, many individuals within our communities are involved as representatives of groups and communities on committees and steering groups that may be more hierarchical. This can be called **vertical participation**. Here their role is to take forward the groups' views and to act as a representative of that community or group. Also they should be taking back information, and decisions that have been made at these meetings to the groups they represent.

Government initiatives are aiming to involve community members in decision making with regard to policy and resource allocation, such as the young people's panels which are distributing Youth Opportunities Funding in England. Similarly there have been moves to involve communities through the setting of local priorities and the distribution of funding, a process referred to as participatory budgeting.

> *Participatory budgeting establishes a process in which the effects of people's involvement are directly seen in either policy change or spending priorities. It is not just a consultation exercise, but an embodiment of direct, deliberative democracy . . . it is a mechanism of local government, which brings local communities closer to the decision-making process around the public budget . . . It is a flexible process, which has been implemented in varying forms across cities of all sizes. It works to enhance participation in local democracy whilst improving community cohesion and ensuring the delivery of cost-effective local services. (Participatory Budgeting Unit DCLG 2007, see www.participatorybudgeting.org.uk)*

Spaces for participation

It is important that we understand the different types of groups and the need for spaces for participation in order to help us to be more effective in our support for community participation.

The table below gives some examples of **horizontal** spaces where community members may be involved in groups and decision making, which I have termed community created spaces. The others are examples of **vertical** spaces or what I have called manufactured spaces. The concept of manufactured civil society was discussed by Hodgson (2004) as the process of non-statutory organizations within the community and voluntary sector taking on what were previously statutory roles.

The table below provides examples of the places where a community member is involved within an inner city area of Manchester, Whalley Range. The table shows the groups they are involved with as representative of the community, whether they felt participation actually took place, and what was achieved by their involvement in relation to benefit to the community.

From analysing the table it can be seen that there is the potential for higher levels of participation within community created and controlled spaces as manufactured spaces often have:

- direction and control by non community members (for example the police, ward coordinators);
- issues formalized through a structured agenda;
- a chairperson that is not usually a community member and is all-powerful, e.g. they determine who is invited, who is enabled to speak and be listened to, and the format of the meeting;
- meetings taking place when and where it suits workers not community representatives, e.g. within work time, in the town hall;
- formal structures which exclude space for deliberation and discussion;

Table 6.1 Spaces for Participation

Space for participatory involvement	Participation taken place	Achievements in relation to community aims
Manufactured spaces:		
Ward coordination	Yes, through representatives at quarterly meetings	Influenced the delivery of services, by helping identify needs, etc.
Primary Care Trust (PCT)	Yes, local people involved in local area groups (LAGs), and through local Health Forum. Currently no participation in PCT	Influenced delivery of services, and identification of local needs. LAGs disbanded and local health development workers terminated with no consultation
Police, local area partnerships/neighbourhood policing	Yes, through local group representation, and links to Home/Neighbourhood Watch schemes	Some, mainly at a local level. Major issues not tackled. Supposed reduction in local crime, etc.
Community Network for Manchester	Yes, through geographical networks and thematic networks, Manchester wide events	Geographical and Manchester wide networks increased, and self help activities. Influence a struggle, affected by lack of resources and limited access of CN4M to Local Area Partnership
Strategic regeneration framework	Partly	Little (see table below)
Community created spaces:		
Whalley Range Community Forum	Yes, through regular meetings, information sharing, newsletter, website and directory and community events	Some, limited by lack of resources, and influence
Many other community groups within the area	Yes, Regular meetings and events, e.g. residents' groups	Same

- community members attending in their own, unpaid time, on a voluntary basis; most others present will be participating as a requirement of their paid work.

Community created spaces can also restrict participation if they are controlled and controlling, however the likelihood of meaningful participation will be restricted in all spaces if the above factors that can reduce community participation are not considered and acted upon.

From the table above it can be seen what was achieved by the involvement of the community members within each of the groups. It is important that the benefit for the individuals and their communities is recognized, as well as the cost (for example in relation to the time that is given for free) of involvement in groups and communities. Part of the role of the worker involved in enabling participation should be to facilitate informal education with the participants, so that they can think critically about their involvement in different types of groups, and how best they can bring about change and improvement.

These processes have been recognized in an evaluation of the learning that has resulted from the Active Learning for Active Citizenship programmes:

> In the interests of developing a citizenship that is both active and critical, it is important that 'horizontal involvement', for example, participation in community groups and networks, needs to be linked to 'vertical involvement', for example, critical and active involvement in wider local and regional forums and formal consultations with (local, regional and national) government. (Johnston, 2008, p.26)

To help us work sensitively and effectively with communities members involved in participation if is helpful to analyse the type of involvement they have.

ACTIVITY *6.2*

Using the framework below identify different types of groups or structures that community members may be involved with. You can do this by thinking about your own involvement as a community member, or where you are working with communities, or draw on other workers' experiences.

Type of group	Horizontal participation	Vertical participation
Manufactured (formed)	1	3
Community created (natural)	2	4

This exercise should show that not all groups that are formed are hierarchical and that some natural groups formed within the community may be involved in vertical participation. For example in box (1) this could be a multi agency steering group including representatives of local groups and service providers working on a shared task.

In box (2) a community created, non hierarchical space, this could be a cooperative or self help group. In box (3), in the manufactured, hierarchical group, this could be a structured formal committee such as local authorities, and ward coordination groups. Box (4) may be a community forum that is run on structured, hierarchical lines.

Being an effective worker

In addition to understanding how groups function and the ways that people may participate in different types of groups, it is important that we understand the importance of participation to the informal education process that is central to our role (as identified in Chapter 2).

As a worker under pressure from funders and managers to obtain outcomes and measurable outputs, it is tempting to consider undertaking much of the work in the community ourselves. This is also sometimes quicker, as contacting other people, to facilitate their work, is a slow process.

However, participation is important because:

1. Individual and group capacity building will be restricted without the range of learning experiences that participation brings.

2. The participants will be experts in their own area and have local knowledge and valuable skills that without their involvement may be overlooked.

3. Self identified needs are more reliable than perceived needs.

4. Community identified responses to those needs are often more appropriate and so more effective.

The Community Development Foundation, when discussing how to 'achieve better community development' (2007), states that the two main purposes for the worker should be:

1. Improving the quality of community life (e.g. economic, social, environmental, cultural) and service development, and enhanced governance –'a citizens community' (Barr and Hashagen, 2007, p.25)

2. Community empowerment.

The four dimensions of the process of community empowerment are:

• Personal empowerment, leading to a learning community;

• Positive action, resulting in a fair and just community;

• Community organizing and volunteer support, resulting in an active and organized community;

• Participation and involvement leading to an influential community. (ibid.)

Case studies from community groups have shown that all too often workers come into communities, take on roles and responsibilities, often promise funding that does not materialize, then leave, not having benefited the community. This has also been seen to be the case where statutory bodies may establish consultative forums, even when a community created forum already existed and needed support. In this situation the forum with immediate access to officers, councillors and resources may supplant the community led forum, resulting in the decline and eventual closure of the community led activity.

Workers may lose sight of their accountability to the community and to their profession, and feel pressurized into meeting the outcomes required of their employer or managers.

CASE STUDY

The enthusiastic worker

Chris has taken on the role of community development worker for a diverse inner city area Sure Start team. Chris does not live locally, but has experience of working in inner city communities. Chris has a standard remit, the same as others across the city, and is expected to work with other providers for children and families in the area, and to meet the standard requirements of the 'core offer'. The new Sure Start centre was built despite community consultation saying overwhelmingly that people wanted support to be given to local groups in a number of hubs, not a centralized service. The concern is that resources will now go into the new centre rather than to support struggling community groups. Chris and other local workers meet monthly to discuss the progress of the centre. No feedback is given to the community, nor apparently any notice taken of the community's wishes.

ACTIVITY 6.3

If you were a youth and community worker in such a Sure Start programme, how could this have been done differently to enable community participation? How would you have been able to make this process of participation an informal education process for the participants?

Using the four dimensions of the community empowerment process as set out above how could this have been done differently?

To be able to undertake this task may have required you to change the way you view those with whom you work. You have to accept that you are not an expert and know best, but you should aim to be an expert informal educator and understand that your role is to facilitate others. You must make the shift from doing 'for', on behalf of people, or doing 'to' people, where they are the objects of actions and have no choice, to doing 'with' as a partner or ally.

Alison Gilchrist identifies the multiple roles that workers need to adopt including acting as a 'bridge', 'holding the door open', and acting as a 'go between', so that people can act 'independently to make and manage their own web of connections' (Gilchrist, 2001, p.116). To enable this we can make safe spaces and provide background knowledge and information. 'The Community Development Challenge', drawing on the national Occupational

Standards for Community Development, states that the worker should enable participation and sustainable communities by working with people in communities to plan for change and take collective action (2006, p.14).

Individual, task and atmosphere factors in participation

Having discussed the types of places where community members may participate, the processes that take place within groups, and identifying the importance of participation in our work as informal educators, it is important that we identify what may be the blocks and barriers to participation and how to overcome these.

Previous discussion in this chapter has explored different types of community participation and the role of the worker in relation to participation in different types of groups. The exercise below will help you to identify the factors that can enable community participation in general.

ACTIVITY 6.4

Enabling participation and identifying blocks and barriers

Think about a recent public event that has taken place in your community. This could be a public meeting, something at school, a council consultation event. Please consider what helped or hindered you when attending that event.

Types of factors	Helped you in attendance/involvement	Hindered or prevented your involvement
Practical/personal	e.g. there was a crèche	e.g. no childcare
The activity itself	e.g. I wanted to find out about local plans	e.g. didn't understand what it was about
Your familiarity and sense of belonging	e.g I arranged to meet a friend there	e.g never been in the building before

---

The three themes in the left column in the task table equate to the types of factors or needs that are usually associated with the requirements for effective group or team work.

They are called firstly the **individual** factors or needs, secondly those associated with the actual **task** itself and thirdly the maintenance or **atmosphere** factor. In group and team analysis these categories are used to identify particular types of roles that people may take on within the life or activities of groups. For example someone who is organized and summarizes what is taking place would be seen to be supporting the task of getting the job done in the group. Someone who makes sure that there is a comfortable atmosphere, perhaps by cracking 'ice breaking jokes', would be enabling a good atmosphere or the maintenance of the group. Someone who listens effectively, gives and receives feedback, would be seen to be supporting the individual participation of those in the group.

Likewise, these factors can be seen to influence people's levels of community participation. Once people attend groups, meetings or events all three types of needs or factors will need to be met so that individuals can participate effectively to help the meeting group carry out its task.

To enable people to reach the point of attending, the same factors also have to be considered. Often we consider the practical or task focused factors that may hinder people's participation, such as lack of child care, or accessible venues, without considering the other two important factors: how people are made to feel welcome and comfortable, and their individual concerns or feelings about what is taking place.

Individual or motivating factors need to be taken into account. For example, people have to feel ownership of the task, be involved in the identification and process of the activity, and see there is some benefit and outcome for them either directly or indirectly, meaning that there should be some change evident. Community members want to see the product of consultations and information, and do not just want to be consulted or informed. Otherwise, they will lose interest.

For example, the volunteers from community groups in Hattersley who carried out a community audit with all community and voluntary groups in their area were not prepared to disseminate the final report until they were able to include the actions that the Neighbourhood Partnership had agreed to take as a result of the group's findings and recommendations. As a result, a steering group of representatives from local groups is now responsible for assessing and allocating small grants to aid local groups.

We also have to be aware of the institutional and societal factors that may make participation difficult if not impossible, for example poverty, technical exclusion (e.g. no recourse to public funds), physical isolation and discrimination. We have to listen to people to find out what prevents them from participating, for example, the time and place of meetings. If they are council officers, will they come in the evening or at weekends, and will the meeting be in the local area rather than in the town hall?

From the factors outlined above it can be assumed that possible participants will carry out their own individual 'cost benefit analysis' of what is worth getting involved in, considering the individual, group and task elements for each activity requiring their involvement. This will be the same for both manufactured and self determined spaces, although in self determined spaces there may be higher levels of satisfaction with the group, for example, if friends or neighbours are involved.

Even though we may be able to remove the practical barriers that may discourage people's participation, for people to want to participate, the activity must be meaningful for them and ideally (unless the atmosphere and individual needs have been met extremely well by the group activity) some change must be possible as a result of their participation.

Conclusion

This chapter has shown the complexity of community participation and raised issues about the role of the Youth and Community Worker in relation to different types of participatory spaces and has identified some of the barriers to participation and what can be done to overcome these. The need to recognize the importance of inclusive and representative participatory practice is discussed in Chapter 7.

I have made the case that we have an important role in enabling effective participation, both for the benefit of active citizens, communities generally and civil and civic society. Participatory research into what helps participation in six locations in the UK and South America recommended that 'facilitating organizations (and workers) that believe that the (community) can be decision makers and protagonists and who will support rather than substitute for them can make an important difference to maintaining meaningful participatory dynamics' (ICPS, 2008, p.67).

We therefore have an important role to empower communities to have a voice and influence within their communities and in relation to the factors that shape their lives. This can be done through the facilitation of participation both on an individual and group level by the enabling of space for 'deliberation':

> *Participation encourages people to feel part of society, to form public opinion, to strengthen public space and respectful social interaction. However these are also qualities that make it attractive to the status quo. Participation can also create an illusion, an illusion that voices are heard without any guarantee that anything will change as a result. What makes participation meaningful . . . is that change must be possible as a result of participation. (ICPS, 2008, p.66)*

REFERENCES

Arnstein, SR (1969) A ladder of citizen participation. *JAIP*, 35 (4): 216–224.

Barr, A and Hashagen, S (2007) *Achieving better community development: ABCD handbook and trainers resource pack.* London: Community development Foundation.

Crick, B (1998) *Education for citizenship and the teaching of democracy in schools.* London: Qualifations and Curriculum Authority.

Department of Communities and Local Government (DLCG) (2006) *The community development challenge.* West Yorkshire: DCLG publications www.communities.gov.uk

Department of Communities and Local Government (DLCG) (2007) *Local Government and Public Involvement in Health Act 2007*. London: DCLG.

Department of Health (2004) *The Children Act. 'Every Child Matters'*. London: Department of Health

Dunn, A, Foot, J, Gaventa, J and Zipfel, T *(2007)* Champions of participation: Engaging citizens in local governance. Report, Institute of Development Studies: University of Sussex Brighton.

Freire, P (1972) *Pedagogy of the oppressed*. London: Penguin Books.

Gilchrist, A (2001) *Working with networks and organizations in the community*, in LD Richardson and M Wolfe, eds, Principles and practice of informal education. London: RoutledgeFalmer.

L Hodgson (2004) Manufactured civil society: counting the cost. *Critical Social Policy*, 79, 24(2): 139–164. London: Sage.

International Centre for Participation Studies (ICPS) (2008) Here the people decide. Research briefing. Bradford: ICPS, Bradford University.

Johnston, R (2008) Re-viewing the active learning for active citizenship model, in J Annette and M Mayo, eds, *Active learning for active citizenship?* Nottingham: NIACE.

Ledwith, M (1997) *Participation in transformation*. Birmingham: Venture Press.

Putnam, RD (2000) *Bowling alone: The collapse and revival of American community*. New York: Simon and Schuster.

Richardson, LD and Wolf, M eds, *Principles and practice of informal education*. London: RoutledgeFalmer.

Take Part (2006) *The national framework for active learning for active citizenship*. London: Department of Communities and Local Government.

Thompson, N (2001) *Anti-discriminatory practice*. Basingstoke: Palgrave Macmillan.

Tuckman, B W and Jensen, MAC (1977) Stages of small group development revisited. *Group and Organizational Studies*, 2, 419–427.

WEBSITES

www.participationworks.org.uk

www.participatorybudgeting.org.uk

www.takepart.org

Chapter 7
Inclusive and representative practice

Introduction

This chapter discusses the importance of ensuring that participation and community involvement are available to all community members not only those who are already in positions of power and privilege, or those who are targeted at being most in need of attention. The concept of citizenship is critiqued recognizing that it can be controlling and excluding as well as potentially empowering, and a framework for inclusive and representative practice is discussed.

Exploring our relations to those with whom we work, the structures and processes that impact upon us, developing an awareness of their impact, and enabling the empowerment of groups and individuals to enable change and transformation at an individual, community and structural level is central to Youth and Community Work practice. Our work has been influenced by popular educationalists such as Paulo Freire (1921–1997), who linked individual education and consciousness raising to issues of power and oppression at a structural level. These processes cannot take place without a commitment to 'promoting equality and valuing diversity' (see the Occupational Standards for Youth Work, and Community Learning and Development (LLLUK, 2008), and social justice, self determination and participation (DCLG, 2006, p.14). This necessitates that we acknowledge that we as workers are adopting a critical perspective based on a social model of practice. To consider factors at community, political and socio-economic levels indicates that we are not individualizing and problematizing those with whom we work.

Inclusive and representative practice is therefore not only one of the key characteristics of informal education; it is also the location of debates surrounding citizenship and active citizenship education.

This book has already discussed dilemmas for practitioners in relation to the role of government in the third sector and in relation to voluntary activity. This chapter will discuss the requirement for active community based learning to challenge also the perspectives evident in some government policies and initiatives that have sought to classify and divide citizens, and identify particular groups of citizens as being targets for intervention.

Gilchrist stated the following in *Equalities and Communities, Challenge Choice and Change: A Handbook for Practitioners*:

Community development in the 21st century is clear about its commitment to equality and human rights. Its fundamental values include participation, empowerment and social justice. Community development has a distinctive role to play in 'overcoming poverty and disadvantage' using a bottom up approach to identifying inequalities and work with communities to address oppression and discrimination, based on a human rights approach (see 'The Community Development Challenge' 2006). Government programmes under New Labour have been underpinned by an increasing concern with social inclusion, community cohesion and citizen empowerment. (Gilchrist, 2007, p.4)

ACTIVITY **7.1**

Identifying barriers to inclusion

You are involved in supporting a community forum in a diverse multi-ethnic community. Although 29 per cent of the population is of Asian origin, participatory research has shown that only 9 per cent of the participants in community meetings are people of Asian origin, and most of these are men. Consider what could be the explanations for the lack of participation in the community. Ensure that you consider individual, community, organizational and structural/social factors.

Your thinking should have shown that barriers to inclusion are not necessarily to do with the individual who is not participating, but that there will be barriers at an organizational, cultural and societal level that may hinder participation in activities. This was evident in the findings of the GEM project outlined below. The project team set out to find out who participated in decision making within Manchester, from the community to city level, and what the barriers were to participation. The team of community researchers, trained in participatory research, found that the barriers to participation in decision making processes were at a personal, cultural/organizational and structural level. Their analysis of participation in meetings, focus group discussions and questionnaires is set out in the case study.

CASE STUDY

The GEM (Gender and Community Engagement in Manchester) project's research findings into reasons for lack of participation in democratic processes

Personal barriers: some were common to both sexes, such as lack of interest or lack of time, other areas were much higher for women, e.g. lack of child care and domestic responsibilities (52 per cent women, 20 per cent men) and issues of personal safety. Isolation and lack of social networks were general barriers to involvement in meetings and decision making forums.

Cultural and organizational barriers: such as inflexible and inappropriate timing of meetings, choice of venue, transport and 'difficult location' (22 per cent women, 8 per cent men). Language used in meetings: for example the use of jargon and style and language of publicity/information. Young people did not feel welcome at meetings and in community processes.

Inefficiency of meetings and processes: 'a waste of time' (30 per cent men, 9 per cent women).

Structural barriers: gender roles acted as barriers, for example women's 'traditional' and cultural roles in relation to immediate and extended family and domestic work, plus intimidation by confident males in social settings (and cultural barriers to, and in mixed sex settings). Young men felt more a part of their communities than young women (67 per cent compared to 27 per cent young women). However, for those aged over 55 twice as many women as men had a sense of belonging and felt part of their communities (42 per cent women, 25 per cent men).

(Berry and Oteyza, 2005)

Setting the context of our work

Youth and Community Work is all too often expected to resolve issues and work with those that are seen as at risk or a risk to themselves, their communities and society. Funding for youth and community projects has followed street riots and rising antisocial behaviour reports. However, little is done to explore the causes of such dissatisfaction and alienation. We are increasingly expected to give advice and guidance to young offenders and NEET young people (those now targeted as not in education, employment and training), to engage people in democratic systems through youth councils and local forums, to provide positive and diversionary activities which make our societies more cohesive. However, we must never lose sight of our role to enable awareness and critique of the structures and processes that create the conditions in which we live and practise. As the findings of the GEM project show, although there are practical, individual factors that act as barriers to participation, issues at an organizational and structural level also need to be tackled to enable participation.

> *Ensuring gender balance in decision making is crucial to social inclusion and to improving people's quality of life. Discussions with local people from different ethnic backgrounds, age, sexuality and areas captured ideas for new channels of participation that would acknowledge gender difference. If implemented, they could lead to decision making that reflected the needs and concerns of men and women equally, for the well-being of the whole community. (Berry and Oteyza, 2005, p.1)*

Recognition of the part played by social divisions and social structure is central to the emphasis on empowerment and social justice evident in Youth and Community Work practice. Thompson (2001) identified three levels at which social interaction took place and hence social divisions were shaped. In his PCS analysis he referred to the **p**ersonal/psychological level (including practical elements and prejudice), **c**ultural and institutional level (including conforming, and consensus to norms) and structural/social divisions level (including socio-political patterns or power and influence) (Thompson, 2001).

Youth and Community Work professionals explore inequality at all three of the PCS levels through methods such as social and political education. This has at times differentiated them from other professions such as social work where the focus of the worker has traditionally been on the individual problems of the 'client'. However, Thompson states

> *where the psychodynamic focus of traditional social work has been criticized for its failure to take account of the social dimensions . . . Social work theory has now progressed to a level of sophistication at which the part played by social divisions and social structure is receiving increasing attention . . . what is needed is a clearer understanding of how problems . . . can be located in this wider structural context.*
> *(Thompson, 2001, p.21)*

Whilst social work has moved towards a recognition of the three levels of social interaction, going beyond purely individual explanations, Youth and Community Work is now at risk of being drawn to the individual (P) and organizational (C) level as the result of changing emphasis on who we work with and how, and increasing organizational and social policy requirements and constraints.

If we are to be effective Youth and Community Workers it is therefore essential that we must:

1. be aware of who we are and understanding of our own perspective, identity and impact;

2. work within the value base and ethics of our profession as discussed in Chapter 2;

3. adopt a social justice and anti-discriminatory approach;

4. aim to achieve inclusive, representative, empowering practice;

5. identify the barriers to achieving this;

6. work collectively to remove these, and bring about change and transformation.

These stages were outlined by the National Youth Work Agency (1995) as the process of group work around particular curriculum areas. The suggested curriculum areas include consideration of education, environment, family and relationships, justice, equality and health. The worker's role in this process being to:

*   facilitate a group work process identifying an issue or area for discussion and change;

*   help young people become aware of the factors involved in the area for consideration;

*   raise questions and seek solutions;

*   identify ways of taking action.

Building on Kolb's (1984) learning cycle this process becomes ongoing. The stage of raising awareness and asking questions involves consideration of the issues at the personal, cultural and societal levels, to help understand the 'why' of the issue. This process of enabling learning is further discussed in Chapters 2 and 8.

Empowering practice

Thompson discusses how empowerment is an essential feature of good practice, whereby the worker enables people to 'gain power and control over their own lives and circumstances . . . to help people to have a voice . . . so that they counter the negative affects of discrimination and marginalization' (2005, p.170).

Batsleer discusses the artificial distinction between personal/individual empowerment which is based more on models of self help and consumerism, and those that are based on 'a collective model of resistance to structures of oppression' (Batsleer, 1996, p.20). Although these approaches can be seen to equate to political approaches (the individual approach having more resonance to the Conservative and New Right and the collective to Socialist and old Labour approaches), Batsleer states that 'this individual/structural dichotomy prevents an analysis of the social, and prevents the recognition that all power, even when it is exercised by individuals, derives from the social order' (ibid., p.20), and is sanctioned by it, and unequally distributed through it.

Part of the role of the worker is to enable those that we work with, through informal education processes and actions, to understand the elements of the social world and their place within it. Freire's (1972) view was that people would not be able to take action to transform the world and their lives unless they could critically analyse and understand the processes within that world, what he called the process of conscientization or becoming aware.

However, not all individuals have the same potential for influence and change. This is dependant upon individual, practical and structural or political factors. Gilchrist identifies psychological, practical and political factors as a basis for a framework for developing what she calls 'equalities-based practice'. She outlines that the worker's aim is to 'find the tools and techniques for working with communities to promote equality and tackle discrimination, to achieve social change at individual, community, institutional and social level . . . (through) a basic commitment to fairness and social inclusion' (Gilchrist, 2007, p.1).

The work of the Active Learning for Active Citizenship programme discussed in the case studies in this book has incorporated community based empowering approaches to learning. As stated by the coordinator of the national pilot programme:

> *empowerment is not something that is done to participants, rather it is a more subtle process whereby people come to recognize their own situation and develop the ability to do something about it. In order to participate and have their voice heard, citizens need to understand power and how to have an impact. Because citizens act together, they need to know and understand something of the conditions of other citizens to support collective action . . . As participants reflect on and review their learning in active citizenship their individual social capital will increase and thereby their confidence and ability to contribute to the social capital of the communities with which they identify. (Woodward, 2004, p.11)*

Inclusive practice and difference

Although social inclusion is often cited as one of the aims of Youth and Community Work, and is increasingly seen as the rationale for their work by policy makers, social inclusion is a controversial and often divisive process, for example, when the needs or requirements of specific groups are ignored. Inclusive practice should refer to an approach where workers take responsibility for enabling people to participate in a way that is chosen by the participants. This requires that we must review, change and adapt our practices. To be able to do this may require a shift in our thinking, our view of the world, making a paradigm shift so that we can see how dominant norms and practices exclude those who are being marginalized.

A combination of factors may lead to a lack of inclusive practice: physical and practical barriers, structural and institutional factors which may be hidden as well as obvious, societal influences such as stereotypes and prejudices, and individual factors which may be exacerbated as a result of these socio-political forces.

To be inclusive means that we have to recognize and value diversity, and not with the aim that people become assimilated into the dominant norms and cultures.

> *Valuing diversity is the moral and professional requirement to recognize and respond to the significant differences of culture, language, gender and so on. These differences are important aspects of interpersonal interactions, for without due sensitivity to their differences the potential for effective and appropriate interactions is seriously reduced.*
> *(Thompson, 2005, p.166)*

Differences and social divisions in the main do not fragment society as 'social divisions interconnect and institutional processes constrain' (Payne, 2006, p.352). However, rather than being celebrated for the contribution that difference makes to communities, differences can become divisive social divisions when they are sustained by dominant cultural beliefs, reinforced by powerful institutions and backed by negative social sanctions. Social divisions are exacerbated by world events and community pressures, and if difference is viewed negatively, for example through bonding capital (Putnam, 2000), it can lead to discrimination and oppression.

ACTIVITY **7.2**

Can you identify a group of people who have been negatively labelled because of their 'difference'? How is this reinforced, what can you do to challenge this?

Government policy and difference

Government policy has focused on 'community' as the source of skills and knowledge as well as being the foundation of a stable and cohesive society. Workers who work within and with communities now have additional expectations placed upon them from government policy and funders. Not only can communities be supported to identify and meet their own needs, but they are now involved in the formation and delivery of policy and service provision, and in making cohesive and safe places to live.

We also have to consider whether government policy is exacerbating social divisions through unequal treatment of communities that are different to the dominant norms of society, or who are not yet viewed by some as citizens, for example asylum seekers, lesbian, gay and young people. Payne argues that without an analytical approach that recognizes social inequalities and injustices, and the way that institutions constrain us (e.g. through social policy and funding constraints), and how different identities are socially created, we will not be able to 'understand, let alone change, the nature of contemporary society and the lives of its citizens' (Payne, 2006, p.359). Thompson places this understanding at an ontological (theoretical) level, and states that this has to be done as a 'basic starting point for tackling inequality discrimination and oppression at the broader socio-political levels. If people are not supported in casting off the shackles of socialization into disempowered roles and frames of reference, it is unlikely they will be able to achieve empowerment at a broader socio-political level' (Thompson, 1998, p.211).

We can enable people to understand the world so that they have the potential to change it, the process of what Freire (1972) called conscientization, or becoming more aware. 'Conscientization can be seen as the process of helping to make people aware of the broader context of the situations they face, and 'politicization' in turn is the process of seeking to address the problems at the broader socio-political level' (Thompson, 1998, p.214).

To counter social exclusion and discrimination, Youth and Community Workers must recognize the impact of these factors on peoples lives, ensure that we do not reinforce such discrimination and oppression, and importantly that we must 'challenge and undermine the oppressive structures, and attitudes and actions that disadvantage certain groups in society' (Thompson, 2005, p.166). This is helped if we think critically about workers' interventions as discussed in the chapter on reflective practice, and work within the ideological framework and principles of our practice as discussed in Chapters 2 and 8.

Representative practice

The term 'representative Youth and Community Work practice', refers to the process of ensuring that our practice reflects and takes into account the compositions of the groups and communities with whom we are working, or are based. It does not mean that these participants will be able to represent these communities, as they may belong to many different communities (e.g. be Polish, a woman, a lesbian), and may not know the views and opinions of the other members of these communities. However, we are more likely to be able to reduce exclusion and achieve social justice if we have attempted to enable as many sections of our communities to have a voice as possible. Without this aim we are merely perpetuating the existing norms, practices and power imbalances within our communities.

Aiming for representative practice is therefore important for three reasons.

Firstly, if we undertake work that has not sought to get the views of or to include representation from all sections of the community, we could be deemed to have been biased, and to have ignored the views or needs of those who have not been involved. This does not mean that in all the work that we do we must seek to get representation from all of the different sections of the community. For example if a group of older people wants to access educational facilities, it might not be appropriate to try to get representatives from young people. However, different sections of older people should be contacted, for example, both men and women, from all ethnicities, religions, sexualities, impairments. To enable this you have to use inclusive practice methods, for example, considering when and where the activities are held, how they are advertised, etc. These issues are discussed in more detail in Chapter 6.

Secondly, if we do not seek to ascertain the views and needs of all sections of the community the services we may provide may be inappropriate, or ineffective, and sections of the community may have their needs and requirements unmet.

Thirdly, without actively seeking to include the diverse sections of our communities, we are leaving untapped the potential of skills, knowledge and abilities of those who are not participating. In relation to democratic engagement this has been called a democratic deficit. When writing about the GEM project outlined above, Berry and Oteyza (2005) suggest that whilst 'making up half of the population, women's full and equal representation is both a question of social justice and a requirement of democracy as well as of full use of human resources, and their under-representation in decision making is a loss for the whole of society and an unacceptable democratic deficit' (European Action Plan, 1996–2000).

The implications of adopting representative practice is that we must be inclusive and take proactive steps to access all sections of the community where appropriate. We should record who takes part to show who we have involved and how representative our work and activities are. We must not make assumptions about requirements, and should make sure that work is based on voiced and felt needs, not what we and others perceive to be the case. By our work being more inclusive and representative we will be developing the full capacity of the community, not perpetuating the same, limited participation and opportunities for action. We will also be contributing to the development of bridging social capital (Putnam, 2000), by enhancing community conversations and understanding.

Citizenship and social inclusion

In the same way that inclusive practice has the potential to control and smother individual and group differences if assimilation as opposed to the social justice approach is adopted, debates around citizenship have also evidenced the contrasting role of citizenship to either increase power or influence, or to exclude those who are not viewed as citizens, for example, by 'no recourse to public funds' for asylum seekers in Great Britain.

Consideration of inclusion and exclusion are therefore particularly important and challenging in relation to citizenship. These debates were evident during the development of the citizenship curriculum for schools, and the ALAC core curriculum for adults (Woodward,

2004). All were drawn up following the work of the 1998 Crick Report on 'Education for Citizenship and the Teaching of Democracy in Schools', whose terms of reference were:

> '. . .to include the nature and practices of participation in democracy: the duties, responsibilities and rights of individuals as citizens: and the value to individuals and society of community activity'. (QCA, 1998)

Responsible citizenship requires adherence to legal and national structures, achieved by promoting 'a sense of national identity, unifying different groups . . . and fostering a sense of citizenship' (from Val Rust cited in Heaton and Lawson, 1996, p.5). This notion of engendering a sense of identity is evident in the Crick Report, which states that the aim is 'to find and restore a sense of common citizenship, including a national identity . . . to create common ground between different ethnic and religious identities' (QCA, 1998, p.17 (3.14)). This common ground, being based on multi-cultural understanding and a respect for minorities, 'must respect the laws codes and conventions as much as the majority' (QCA, 1998, pp.17–18 (3.16)). Crick's approach, whilst recognizing the importance of diversity, advocates that this is subsumed into a common national identity, advocating assimilation and conformity, not inclusion based on the rights which should be central to citizenship.

Approaches to citizenship

There are different definitions of citizenship that are evident in educational approaches. Citizenship education is different from education for citizenship: the former implies an ongoing process to enable citizens to engage effectively and productively within the world; the latter implies preparation for a future role within society, for example through proposed citizenship ceremonies or 'new citizens'.

Youth and Community Work practice sees citizenship education as an ongoing process. It uses informal education, with its commitment to the right to participation and negotiation, and an emphasis on inclusion and the challenging of discrimination and oppression. The Youth and Community Work informal education's approach to citizenship therefore adopts a critical perspective which sees citizenship as linked to empowerment of the individual and communities and therefore to the potential for change. That is 'citizenship as participation represents an expression of human agency in the political arena' (Lister, 1997, p.35).

A rights based, 'liberal' approach

This approach to citizenship education supports the liberal tradition that sees citizenship as synonymous with the possession of rights. This approach can be illustrated by social policy in relation to formalizing the rights of children. The application of the 1989 Children Act within schools has

> significantly strengthened the position of children . . . it translates as a form of pupil empowerment which has been externally imposed and legitimated. Primacy is given to the views, wishes and feelings of individual pupils, investing them with legal rights, enabling them to challenge teacher authority and school practices. (Irving and Parker-Jenkins, 1995, p.3)

These rights have been further enshrined in the five areas of 'Every Child Matters', set out in the Children Act 2004. This states that all young people from birth to 19 should be supported to be healthy, stay safe, enjoy and achieve, make a positive contribution and achieve economic well-being.

These aims have been further developed by the ten year strategy for young people, 'Aiming High':

> *The government's vision is for all young people to enjoy happy, healthy and safe teenage years that prepare them well for adult life and enable them to reach their full potential – in short, to achieve the five* Every Child Matters *outcomes and be on the path to success. Young people should be valued members of society, whose achievements and contributions are welcomed and celebrated. This means society viewing young people positively, not seeing them as a problem to be solved . . . While this vision applies to all young people, action to deliver it should be focused on providing support and opportunities to those for whom this vision will be hardest to achieve. (DfCSF, 2007, p.8)*

The functionalist, responsibilities led approach

In contrast to the rights based 'liberal' approach discussed above, the functionalist account views education for citizenship as the production of responsible citizens. This links to the republican tradition which associates citizenship with the 'pursuit of the good for a particular community' (Batsleer and Humphries, 2000), thus being about the assimilation of law abiding, dutiful and productive citizens. The process through which this is achieved is by work. The functionalist approach emphasizes the role of schools in the preparedness for work, and also implies that to be without work (and so become the recipient of welfare and dependent on the state) is a failure of citizenship (Batsleer and Humphries, 2000).

This functionalist approach to citizenship draws on Marshall's (1950) definition of citizenship, which stated that 'citizenship was a status conferred upon people with full membership of a community . . . who received an equality in respect to certain rights and duties'. This implies that citizenship is not assumed as a right as the result of participation in a society, but that it has to be given, or earned. Feminist and other critics of Marshall have argued that his definition does not take into account the interdependence of citizens as a necessity for the fulfilment of their rights and responsibilities as autonomous citizens, and that young people and others who may not be contributing to society (e.g. through work) are citizens not merely the recipients of welfare.

Youth and Community Work (focusing on the principles of empowerment, participation and inclusion, and carried out through a process of informal social and political education) believes that young people have the rights and ability to be active citizens now, that is within their everyday lives, including school, not merely preparing them for a future role in society.

Contrasting definitions of citizenship such as the liberal and functionalist approaches illustrate the potential for policy to run counter to rights based social inclusion approaches:

Sometimes, these views have been an unintended consequence of government policies to tackle some serious problems affecting the lives of some teenagers. Rather than presenting a positive vision for youth development, national priorities and local services have been organized and targeted around avoiding and addressing problems, such as crime, substance misuse, or teenage pregnancy. While it is right to continue to focus on addressing these issues, and to deal firmly with young people who are causing harm to their neighbourhoods and themselves, it also important to be aware of the influence this has on popular perceptions. ('Aiming High', DfCSF 2007, p.5)

The ten year youth strategy is a good example of contradictory notions of citizenship, in this case in relation to young people

---

CASE STUDY

Aiming High for young people: a ten year strategy for positive activities

The strategy aims to ensure that 'young people are empowered to have influence over, and have access to, high quality positive activities and wider youth support services' (DfCSF, 2007, p.81) in the hope that when young people have the opportunity to influence services, they are more likely to find them attractive and to access and benefit from them. The strategy identifies that 'more marginalized young people can find formal processes unappealing and will need additional support to influence provision' (2007, p.14).

However, despite talking about the empowerment of young people to take the lead in deciding the funding and type of youth activities, and being involved in their communities through volunteering (e.g. through a National Youth Volunteering Programme), the 'Aiming High' strategy still adopts a functionalist approach to young people's citizenship and talks about them 'taking their place in society'. This is to be achieved when they reach adulthood, possibly recognized by a specific citizenship ceremony, so

> *Demonstrating trust in young people's ability to make a valuable contribution and take part in decisions affecting them will send a clear signal about their place in society. It is in the interests of all to take a more positive view of young people and do more to help them take their equal place as citizens. This requires concerted action at local and national level. (2007, p.36).*

Citizenship in this context is not a right but one to be gained through a process of learning what it 'means to be a British citizen . . . and understanding their role and responsibility in society' (ibid.).

The strategy sees active citizenship as a way of social control for young people. It states:

Empowering young people to play a full role as active citizens is essential to improving their relationship with adults in their communities. Concerns about antisocial behaviour are lower where young people are engaging positively in their local communities, for example through volunteering. (2007, p.36)

The PCS model and citizenship

Despite differing approaches as to who and when people are citizens, the Marshall (1950) and Crick (1998) approaches to citizenship education share with Youth and Community Work the three elements identified in the PCS analysis, that is that our interactions take place at a personal, cultural and societal level. The citizenship curriculum in schools refers to these as 'moral responsibility, community involvement and political literacy' (QCA, 1998). These are to be gained through the acquisition of knowledge and understanding (e.g. about the law, the local and global community), and skills and aptitudes (e.g. to be able to work in groups, carry out research, be involved in community based activities, use statistics).

The citizenship curriculum framework recommends that knowledge should be practically acquired and relevant. It therefore would appear to be an initiative closely related to the methods and content of informal education, particularly informal social and *political* education that has for many years sought to enable young people to understand, take part in, and locate themselves within the processes and structures that affect their lives and those of their communities.

As discussed in Chapter 6, the Youth and Community Worker, in order to facilitate group work, needs to be aware of the individual needs and requirements of the participants, and to enable a positive group atmosphere. The participants in any group or community are diverse and what binds them together is the commitment to the task, but 'because people belong to several groups, they have a vested interest in constraining and resolving conflict in any one group' (Payne, 2006, p.354).

> For example a community audit team from the Manchester Refugee Support Forum in Manchester was comprised of a group of 5 men and 7 women, all of whom are asylum seeker or refugees. They were from seven countries and spoke 17 languages in addition to English. They all came from many different communities in relation to identity and neighbourhood/location. However, they were helped to work together in a supportive and productive way around a shared theme of identity and the untapped capacity within the refugee and migrant communities in Manchester.

However, in addition to enabling understanding at a horizontal community level and enabling bridging capital, the worker has a role in facilitating what Payne (2006) calls the ontology (theory) and understanding the socio-political structures that affect our lives and opportunities. Thompson uses the PCS model, which can be compared to the levels of consideration in the citizenship curriculum, and identifies that people are involved in processes at a personal, cultural and structural level. Our role as worker is to facilitate the process of understanding how these three areas are interlinked, and to enable citizens to be empowered to take action. This is the process of popular or informal education as illustrated through the discussion of Schools of Participation in Chapter 2.

As Thompson states '. . . assisting people to take greater control over their lives, can have a significant positive impact on the person level, thereby making a contribution at the cultural (institutional) level and in turn playing at least a small part in undermining inequality at the structural (societal and global) level' (Thompson, 1998, p.212).

CASE STUDY

Citizenship dilemmas and the ALAC programme

The Active Learning for Active Citizenship programme has been an example of a group of workers sharing the same principles, values and methods, working alongside a wide range of community groups to influence policy and practice at a national level. The initial funding for the ALAC programme came from the Home Office and was aimed at the delivery of a citizenship curriculum for adults, enabling people to be better informed community leaders. The aim was to enable communities, particularly those who were 'hard to reach', to be involved in the design of services, and by being active within their communities to increase community cohesion and integration.

It was agreed at the inception of the ALAC programme that our work was not engaging with nationality issues and the newly created citizenship tests for new citizens, but that we were using a rights based approach enabling the empowerment of all regarding their legal status. This distinction became clearer when the reorganization of government departments resulted in our link department becoming the Community Empowerment Division of the newly formed Department for Communities and Local Government, clearly leaving legalistic issues of nationality and citizenship within the Home Office.

The ALAC group adopted a Freirian approach to the work and rejected a set curriculum for active citizenship in favour of informal education processes that enabled groups of community members to be involved in experiential learning through self determined action. Rather than working with specific groups the

> *Key values for this work are therefore social justice, participation, equality and diversity and co-operation . . . providing education for and encouraging active citizenship needs to actively challenge exclusionary attitudes and practices, not just guard against excluding groups or people. Reflection and critical consciousness must be encouraged at all times.*

> *(Woodward, 2004, pp.12–13)*

Models for practice

Knowing who we are

To enable us to be effective practitioners involved in the processes of inclusive and representative practice it is essential that we first identify who we are, and how this affects our practice in relation to our power and influence. Workers like those with whom we work need to have agency as active citizens and to be aware of the choice and influence that we have at the three levels of interactions discussed in this chapter (PCS). This will be influenced by the 'a web of social forces' (Gardner, 2007, p.22) and external social influences dependent upon our social class, sexuality, ethnicity, age impairment, etc. As Gardner states, 'while individuals have a degree of flexibility to exercise their will, they do so within a limited range of possibilities' (2007, p.21). Gardner, like Thompson, discusses how societal factors impact on the individual's identity and agency (ability to take action).

Acting as an empowering and empowered worker

Youth and Community Workers often have little in the way of resources, and who we are, and the skills we possess and apply, are our greatest assets. Knowing who we are will enable us to work alongside some community members whose identities we share and act as allies with others. For example as a woman worker I can facilitate girls' work with a group of young women and act as an ally to my male colleague who is carrying anti-sexist work with boys, by challenging stereotypes and discriminatory language and behaviour.

Every one of us has an important role in relation to facilitating the informal education process at the three levels that have been identified in this chapter (PCS).

Table 7.1 Implementing the PCS model through informal education

	Working to support groups with whom you identify	Working as an ally
Personal/individual action Enable discussion about issues and problems, and possible action at an individual level.	Enable self help activities, share common experiences, consciousness raising and confidence building. Act as a positive role model.	Challenge stereotypes, discriminatory behaviour, and language, facilitate inclusion from a social justice approach. Act as a role model for effective anti-discriminatory practice.
Cultural/institutional action Enable discussion about issues and problems, and possible action at a group, organizational and cultural level.	Work with the group to enable them to identify areas for change e.g. policies and procedures, practices.	Identify what needs to be done to enable inclusion e.g. change activities, staff composition etc. Act as advocates based on what people have said.
Societal/structural action Enable discussion about issues and problems, and possible action at structural, societal and global level. Help understand how socio political and economic factors impact on individuals and groups and what can be done to change this. Raise awareness of different perspectives and how things can be different. Understand the world from a different/new perspective.	Work to empower, make alliances and allies. See all areas of difference as interwoven with other power relations e.g. gender with ethnicity or disability.	Challenge stereotypes, and discriminatory laws, policies and practices.

As can be seen from Table 7.1, the worker has a role to enable discussion and critical dialogue whether carrying out specific work, such as a woman worker carrying out confidence building with women, or working in alliance with a male worker carrying out anti-sexist work with young men.

We can work with the group through the three levels of awareness and possible action. In the table the categories are not mutually exclusive. However, the intention is to help you to think about the different role you may take within different contexts depending on who you are. In some settings and with different groups you may have more power than others. However, you should aim to work through the informal education processes with the group at any opportunity and help them identify areas for change. Applying a structural analysis with groups prevents us from problematizing individuals and particular groups within society and communities. For example, if we take the view that world economic policies have resulted in wars and starvation in some areas, therefore causing people to flee their country and seek asylum within our community, this will lead to a greater understanding of shared issues and human rights.

Thompson (1998) talked about the worker's role in enabling understanding of the impacts and dynamics of power and difference, and the processes of conscientization (awareness) and politicization (the addressing of problems in their sociopolitcal context). In this process Thompson sees the worker as a partner to community members (not seeing themselves as experts and problematizing the community and its members), and a collaborator (what I have called an ally) with others to pursue the challenge of discrimination and oppression using critically reflective practice (as discussed in Chapter 9). These should be collective, transparent and open processes drawing on our professional value base. We should also engage in what Thompson calls 'elegant challenging', the process of skilfully challenging the actions and attitudes of others where these can be seen to be discriminatory or oppressive in their consequences (1998). This is a similar process to that of Batsleer's 'respectful conversation', which takes place within a context of 'working coalitions, of alliances and conversations across difference' (2008, p.19).

Our self awareness therefore has to be the starting point to work in an inclusive and anti-discriminatory way. We must be aware of who we are and careful that our actions are not contributing to the discrimination and oppression that people may experience, for example by the language that we use.

An equalities based approach?

Much national, local and organizational policy is now based on a commitment to equal opportunities. These policies and procedures have been the result of many years of campaigning by pressure groups, for example in relation to discrimination on the grounds of sexuality and disability. However, they may not be enough. Equal opportunities takes as a starting point the dominant norms and practices of society and provides equal opportunities alongside those dominant practices, for example women being given the same pay as men carrying out the same work. A social justice and rights based approach goes beyond equal opportunities and challenges discrimination and exclusion, making the demand that difference has to be recognized and norms and practices changed.

As an example of the perpetuation of the status quo, I will critique the three-factor framework for developing equalities put forward by Gilchrist in *Equalities and communities* (2007). Like the PCS model, she identifies the psychological, practical and political factors that are involved in the way 'our society is organized that maintains power and privilege for some while denying opportunities to others' (2007, p.13), and considers the obstacles and biases that exist as a result and what counter measures can be put in place. However, within this framework there is little evidence of consciousness raising, most of the emphasis being on what can be done practically to enable people's participation. Most importantly there is no evidence of intention to change structures at a 'political' level (i.e. the dominant norms and processes), but ways are suggested to enable people to fit in (e.g. through 'reserved places on forums or committees' (Gilchrist, 2007, p.14)).

Woodward (2008) also identifies the problem, with approaches such as the one proposed by Gilchrist

> that actually focus upon countering supposed deficits amongst participants, accepting and not challenging existing power relationships . . . Communities cannot, and should not, be expected to simply 'pull up their socks' and solve all the problems that they experience by themselves . . . changes in power relationships must be included in policy developments. (Woodward, 2008, p.64)

An alternative approach can be seen in relation to the under-representation of women in decision making. Rather than merely give women space at a meeting where there may be nothing of interest for them to discuss due to the predominant male interests, **gender mainstreaming** 'ensures that women and men have equal access to and control over resources, services and decision-making, at all stages of projects, programmes and policies' (Oteyza, 2006, p.4). To enable this, there has to be a commitment to undertaking change at all three levels, particularly the structural and political levels, and there has to be an awareness of how exclusion takes place. The GEM project therefore carries out gender awareness and anti-sexist training with mixed groups and policy makers, and undertakes single sex work with groups of women, in safe spaces, to help them identify the blocks and barriers to their participation and build their levels of confidence to enable them to take part (see the Take Part learning framework, 2006 for examples of inclusion strategies and how to create safe spaces, e.g. pages 41, 42, 65 at www.takepart.org/framework-for-active-learning).

> We have worked in different ways to create safe spaces where we encourage a 'respectful discourse'; where we can get beyond assumptions around education, work, marriage, sex, tradition, faith, class, age, culture, housework, children, politics and power – where we can 'hear the hurt'. These are spaces for difficult discussions and joint celebrations, spaces to explore what shapes and shaped us and what we want to do about this. (Annette and Mayo, 2008, p.86)

This approach, although recognizing difference, does not prioritize people's experience.

> In the GEM project approach, gender relations were perceived as interwoven with the other power relations of class, ethnicity, religion and age in different contexts. This combination of factors and relations influence everyday experiences and perceptions of women and men in their communities and political structures.

> *A participative process, a two way dialogue between local people and policy makers or service providers, is essential to the articulation of the rights, interests and needs of both women and men (Oteyza, 2008).*

Enabling participation in general has been discussed in Chapter 6. In addition we must be aware of what may exclude people from participating, and take steps to change our practice in order to enable participation. This will involve listening to people's requirements and making sure that we do not further distance and dis-empower people through labelling them as disadvantaged, discriminated against, or dangerous.

In relation to our own practice it is easier and quicker to make change at the personal level where we and the people we work with have most power and influence. However, by raising awareness and showing people that they can influence change either as an individual or through a group or campaign, they will be more likely to be active and engaged citizens.

Conclusion

This chapter has made the case that Youth and Community Workers have an important role to enable people to understand the factors that shape their opportunities, and have agency to act in challenging oppressive forces and making positive change and transformation within their lives. This involves recognizing social difference so that we can take a critical and structural approach to our practice. Batsleer recommends that

> *practices associated with 'active citizenship' and 'community cohesion' needs to begin with plurality, the recognition that young people are as likely as adults to be diverse and divergent in their voices. Otherwise integration will always be promoted on the terms of the dominant group and 'community cohesion' will become another version of 'assimilation'. (Batsleer, 2008, p.247)*

The recognition of plurality and diversity, however, is not straightforward. Controversial research by Robert Putnam in diverse communities has found that there is a decrease in social cohesion within such communities. He suggests that to counter this growing fragmentation 'new cross-cutting forms of social solidarity and more encompassing identities' should be developed to build bridging social capital, a process that he says will be 'speeded by our collective efforts' (Putnam, 2006, np). This does not mean that difference within communities is ignored, but that the process of bonding and bridging capital should be understood and facilitated.

The ALAC programme (now renamed Take Part) is an example of such critical practice which has been able to challenge and influence approaches to citizenship within UK government policy.

> *The Take Part approach is underpinned by the recognition that our society is not equal in terms of money, capital, education, prospects, environments, employment, health and so on. It advocates:*
>
> • *supporting people to challenge attitudes and behaviours of individuals and practices of institutions that discriminate against and marginalize people;*

- *making sure that barriers to attending and taking part are reduced so that learning opportunities are open and inclusive to those who want to take part;*

- *bringing diverse groups of people together and facilitating authentic dialogue around differences and commonalities to try to reduce the perceived barriers between them. (Take Part learning framework, 2006, p.19)*

This chapter has made the case that Youth and Community Workers have an important role to enable these processes. For that to be done successfully without further perpetuating negative social divisions and exclusion it is important that we take an analytical, critical and political approach to practice. This necessitates consideration and action at the personal, cultural and structural levels.

REFERENCES

Annette, J and Mayo M (2008) *Active learning for active citizenship*. Leicester: NIACE.

Batsleer, J (1996) *Working with girls and young women in community settings*. Aldershot: Arena.

Batsleer, J (2008) *Informal learning in youth work*. London: Sage.

Batsleer, J and Humphries, B (2000) *Welfare, exclusion and political agency*. London: Routledge.

Berry, H and Oteyza, C (2005) *Gender and participation*. Manchester: GAP Unit, MMU, Community Audit and Evaluation Centre (see also www.ioe.mmu.ac.uk/CAEC/GAP).

Crick, B (1998) *Education for citizenship and the teaching of democracy in schools*. London: Qualification and Curriculum Authority.

Department for Education and Skills (2004) *Every child matters: Change for children*. London: HMSO, DFES.

Department of Communities and Local Government (DCLG) (2006) *The community development challenge*. West Yorkshire: DCLG publications (www.communities.gov.uk).

Department for Children, Schools and Families (DfCSF) (2007) *Aiming high*. London: DCFS/Treasury.

Freire, P (1972) *Pedagogy of the oppressed*. London: Penguin Books.

Gardner, P (2007) Living and learning in different communities: cross cultural comparisons, in P Zwozdiak-Myers, ed., *Childhood and youth studies*. Exeter: Learning Matters, pp.13–24.

Gilchrist, A (2007) *Equalities and communities, challenge choice and change*. London: Community Development Foundation.

Heaton, T and Lawson, T (1996) *Education and training*, London: Macmillan.

Irving, B and Parker-Jenkins, M (1995) Pupil empowerment: Pupil power. *Pastoral Care*, June, 3–6.

Kolb, D (1984) *Experiential learning: Experience as the source of learning and development*. Englewood Cliffs, NJ: Prentice Hall.

Life Long Learning UK (LLLUK) (2008) *Common standards for community learning and development*. London: Sector Skills Development Agency/LLUK.

Lister, R (1997) Citizenship, towards a feminist synthesis. *Feminist Review*, 57, 28–48.

Marshall, TH (1950) *Citizenship and social class.* Cambridge: Cambridge University Press.

National Youth Agency (1995) *Planning the way,* Leicester: NYA.

Oteyza, C (2006) *Gender and the city*. Manchester: Community Audit and Evaluation Centre MMU.

Oteyza, C. May 2008 Email communication with the author.

Payne, G (2006) *Social divisions.* Basingstoke: Palgrave Macmillan.

Putnam, RD (2000) *Bowling alone: The collapse and revival of American community*. New York: Simon and Schuster.

Putnam, D (2006) Pluribus unum: Diversity and community in the twenty-first century, Johan Skytte Prize Lecture, 2006.

Qualifications and Curriculum Authority (QCA) (1998) *Education for citizenship and the teaching of democracy in schools. The Crick report.* London: DFEE.

Take Part (2006) *The national framework for active learning for active* citizenship. London: DCLG.

Thompson, N (1998) *Promoting equality.* Basingstoke: Macmillan.

Thompson, N (2001) *Anti-discriminatory practice.* Basingstoke: Palgrave.

Thompson, N (2005) Anti-discriminatory practice, in R Harrison and C Wise, *Working with young people.* London: Open University Press/Sage, pp.166–175.

Woodward, V (2004) *Active learning for active citizenship.* London: Home Office.

Woodward,V (2008) *Coordinating the active learning for active citizenship pilots,* in J Annette and M Mayo, *Active learning for active citizenship*. Nottingham: NIACE.

Chapter 8

Community based learning: learning by doing

Introduction

This chapter draws on the characteristics of informal education outlined in Chapter 2, the principles and practices of participation, and inclusive and representative practice identified in Chapters 6 and 7. It clarifies the rationale and importance of community based learning, particularly in relation to the involvement of community members as citizens in civil and civic activities. The discussion locates our work in relation to other types of learning within communities, and clarifies the role of the worker in enabling the learning process. Ways of recognizing learning and outcomes at individual, group and societal level are outlined. Readers are asked to provide a structured framework for a proposed or actual community learning activity, based on the needs, interests and requirements of a group, showing the considerations for effective informal education.

ACTIVITY 8.1

List three things that you have learnt today, for example: if I get up late I miss the bus; biofuels are not good for the environment; next door's car was broken into.

How did you learn this? For example, through personal experience, from the media, through word of mouth/personal contact.

If possible ask someone else to do the same and discuss the different ways that you have learnt this information or skill.

These examples will have shown that

a) learning is an ongoing process and is essential for us to develop, change and grow throughout our lives;

b) acquiring new knowledge or refining existing skills and knowledge can be achieved through many routes, for example via others sharing their learning or experience in formal or informal ways, and through reflecting on your own experience (discussed in more detail in Chapter 9).

As Youth and Community Workers we are involved in a process of facilitating and enabling others' learning through the processes of informal education or what Freire (1970) called popular education. The learning process can take place in any setting with any number of people, applying the characteristics already discussed in Chapter 2, for example discussing with residents about their involvement in meetings and community activities, working with them to prepare, plan, evaluate and feed back. Whatever the context, the elements and dimensions of the educational process should be the same, whether this is in a formed group with a particular task, a natural group in the launderette, or working with individuals. The process may take place within a single conversation or discussion, or as a planned process over a number of weeks.

Informal education in Youth and Community Work

Many texts have been written outlining the elements of the informal education process, for example *Principles and Practice of Informal Education – Learning through Life* (Richardson and Wolfe, 2001). The book discusses how 'people learn from each other in social exchanges which only rarely involve a professional educator' (p.xii). However, if the role of Youth and Community Worker is to be as informal educator, this implies that we are aiming to enable learning and to foster learning environments.

The term 'informal education' is often used when working with young people and rarely in relation to community work. In addition some community work texts, although seeing the value of learning and reflective learning for the practitioner (see Banks et al., 2003), do not necessarily see this as an essential element of learning for the community participant. For example, Twelvetrees' (2002) work is very much about how the worker can help community groups form and function effectively, and how to carry out community profiles.

Others who take a more critical approach to community engagement see the importance of community as a site for learning to take place and a means of generating learning opportunities. Gilchrist (2001) refers to communities as being 'environments for learning', where informal educators can enable communities to create places for the collection of knowledge, where social networks can be shared, and where learning from experience and organizing responses can take place.

In addition, rather than being a reactive process, communities, either geographical or born out of shared interests, can be encouraged to network and identify areas for action. For example, facilitation of a discussion regarding a shared experience of discrimination can help participants discover 'a social or political explanation for their experience and lead to increased confidence' and so become 'agents of their own liberation' (Gilchrist 2001, p.110). It is important that the principles and methods of informal education should be applied to both Youth and Community Work, if only to align the two elements of our profession.

Informal education can take place in a variety of settings, with young people and adults, with individuals and groups, and in structured or unstructured ways. The important defining feature is that the principles of our approach, to enable empowerment, transformation and change, are put into practice.

As a starting point the key characteristics of this process can be identified as

1) providing an informal education opportunity: space;

2) being problem posing not problems solving (aided by reflection);

3) being self determined, in relation to setting, timing and focus;

4) being voluntarily undertaken;

5) having high levels of participation through all stages (from inception to evaluation);

6) being inclusive, based on social justice and anti-discriminatory practice;

7) using critical dialogue;

8) involving working in groups (preferably diverse, sometimes specific around particular themes);

9) encouraging critical thinking, praxis;

10) enabling conscientization, politicization;

11) seeking to improve, transform and change;

12) being a cyclical, ongoing process.

Ledwith's book *Participation in Transformation* is essential reading to understand the application of Freirian informal education principles to community work. Ledwith sees it as being an imperative that we should be engaged in the process to 'carve out the most radical space of possibility in order to make silenced voices heard' (1997, p.147), not only to counter exclusion but also 'to counter global capitalist systems of domination' (ibid.). Her thinking is further explored in *Community Development: A Critical Approach* (Ledwith, 2006). Such a critical approach as that outlined by Ledwith (1997, 2006) and Butcher et al. in *Critical Community Practice* (2007) is therefore essential for ensuring that a social justice approach is central to our work, and that our aim is to empower and transform.

Learning through and in groups

As outlined here the process of collective working and learning as part of a group is an essential element of informal education. The centrality of this is stated in 'the Community Development Challenge', which sets 'working and learning together' (DLGC, 2006, p.14) as being one of the values and principles of community development.

This is similar to what Wenger calls a 'social theory of learning' (2005), which he identifies as being a group work process involving talking about experience using the following components:

• meaning (seeing our life and the world as meaningful);

• practice (identifying what can sustain mutual engagement in action);

• community (recognizing difference and the value of participation);

• identity (understanding how learning changes who we are).

According to Wenger these components have to be integrated 'to characterize social participation as a process of learning and knowing' (2005, p.144) and can take place in any setting, in what he calls 'communities of practice' (ibid.).

As Woodward states, when discussing the requirements for active learning for active citizenship:

> community educators have long advocated that people learn most effectively from their peers and through involvement in action, rather than through abstraction in the classroom, developing critical situations for them to enact, and thus providing a lived experience of the problem under discussion. (Woodward, 2008, p.58)

The process of educational discussion, however, does not remain at the individual level, it moves through stages of awareness raising at a personal, cultural and societal level as discussed in Chapter 7. Learning takes place by reflecting on experience but also through creating opportunities for actual participation and involvement, for example through volunteering and group actions. The worker's role is to 'ensure learning is relevant, purposeful and accessible to people as part of their everyday lives' and to help in 'contextualizing their individual experiences in relation to those of people across Britain, Europe and the world' (Woodward, 2004, p.12).

Community learning and active citizenship

Keeping a focus on the perspectives of informal education is essential with work involving citizenship and active citizens. Government social policy initiatives, as outlined elsewhere in this book, may see learning for citizenship as being a means to socialize citizens, and those hoping to become citizens, into the expected dominant norms and behaviours of society. However, if the informal education processes set out in this text are utilized, the learning that takes place will challenge oppressive structures and processes and empower citizens as part of creative groups and communities.

CASE STUDY

Active Learning for Active Citizenship (ALAC)

The Active Learning for Active Citizenship programme initiated by the Home Office (now re-named as 'Take Part' and supported by the Department for Communities and Local Government) exemplified the tensions and contradictions apparent in some government social policy initiatives. As discussed in Chapter 3, the impetus for the ALAC pilots came from the then Home Secretary David Blunkett who was an advocate of communitarian ideals. However, his methods for engendering engagement within society were focused primarily on the development of civic duty. His draft citizenship curriculum reflected this. Most of the areas of knowledge he required active citizens to acquire concerned knowledge regarding how government at local and national level works, and what policies and procedures existed (for example, data protection). The tensions apparent through the Take Part programme were that the Home Office, as evidenced in the ALAC curriculum, was taking a primarily civic approach to citizenship. It wished to control the content of the training to be provided. It had a focus on individual/human capital through the training of community leaders. Although working through the community and voluntary sector, the programme failed to recognize the need to increase the capacity of these groups as opposed to individuals. The work of the seven pilot projects (the hubs) identified the importance of civil as well as civic involvement and the importance of association for the participants, learning and working as groups. Examples of the ALAC programme included work with women in the Midlands encouraging them to become more active in and on behalf of their communities, and disabled people in the South West of England 'speaking up' and informing service providers of their needs and wishes. The ALAC pilot hub projects saw the set curriculum as being controlling and stifling and failing to respond to particular requirements and settings. The ALAC programme therefore developed a learning framework for ALAC, based on community development and Freirian principles and practice.

Informal education and citizen involvement

Informal education can be seen to have distinctive characteristic elements as outlined above and to have a clear role for the worker. Youth and Community Workers are not necessarily the only people who practise informal education. However, we are the only professionals who are trained to use consistently such principles and approaches across a range of settings with a variety of participants. We are ideally placed to support the learning of community members such as volunteers and active citizens, and to enable their work to lead to the generation of social as well as human and state capital.

The importance of this work is recognized in the occupational standards for Youth and Community Work professionals. The Occupational (Common) Standards for Community Learning and Development (www.lifelonglearninguk.org) and the Professional and Occupational Standards for Youth Work both make a requirement that workers should carry out educational work with groups and enable active citizenship. Section 1.13. states that workers must encourage individuals through community learning and development processes to broaden their horizons and be active citizens, and Section 1.2.3. requires workers to encourage and support others in active citizenship, to be informed and engaged citizens (Life Long Learning UK, 2008, pp.2–3).

The process of informal education in relation to active citizenship can take place on an individual level through unplanned and unstructured engagement, where conversations and discussions may enable learning and new understanding to take place. It can also take place in structured or unstructured group situations. As has been discussed in Chapter 2, the value of work with groups to enable reflection, debate and action is an important element of the informal education process. The skill of the Youth and Community Worker is that these learning opportunities may arise in unplanned ways, such as in the back of a minibus on the way to a trip, where a local incident may become a focus for a discussion regarding how to respond to a rise in violent crime. Or they can be more structured and planned.

As discussed in Chapter 3, fluid unstructured situations are becoming less common, coming under pressure from the desire for outcome driven funding and policy. However, there is still the possibility to use the stages identified as characteristic of the informal education process as identified in this chapter even within the confines of more structured settings and curriculums.

The key components of community learning, and the contribution of community learning to civic and civil involvement, were identified through a European participatory research programme with groups in Ireland, Spain, Bulgaria and Romania into the 'non-formal education processes that underpin democratic activity' (Forrester, 2004, p.5). The research identified key elements in the facilitation of democratic citizenship:

- the requirement for membership and forms of social participation (particularly within your own community);

- control and autonomy over their lives, for example the ability to choose between different courses of action (capacities for action);

- citizenship themes including 'a commitment to human rights for all, commitment to equality and equity in a world of difference, belief in the importance of democratic principles as well as the importance of civil action'. (Forrester, 2004, pp.30–31)

In addition to the key themes their report identifies three characteristics of the learning process:

- 'learning with others' (recognizing the importance of the participant's identity, connected-ness to the community and a sense of agency to achieve something worthwhile);

- 'learning from experience' (based on evaluation or critical reflection);

- 'learning and doing' through collaborative activities undertaken by groups.

All three areas reflect the key themes identified as the characteristics of informal education, critical dialogue, active self directed engagement, and a commitment to a critical, inclusive perspective.

The type of education identified as contributing to citizenship and social and human capital was also identified by Mayo (1997) when discussing the role of adult education in transformation. Drawing on competing theoretical perspectives she stated that

> *at one end of the theoretical spectrum, neo-liberal, New Right debates focus upon the scope for individual entrepreneurs . . . at the other end of the theoretical spectrum, debates focus on the possibilities for both individual and collective action to promote forms of economic and social development which are effectively geared towards combating poverty and deprivation and towards the enhancement of social justice and equal opportunities. (1997, p.3)*

In relation to educational processes these theories underpinned what she termed market led approaches that are geared towards equipping learners with the skills and knowledge required for the workplace. This approach is particularly evident in vocational training schemes. However, they fail to address sources of discrimination and social exclusion. At the other end of the spectrum she groups alternative approaches which place adult education in relation to its contribution in the community in social terms, for example 'promoting active citizenship and democracy' (1997, p.21). Mayo, drawing on the work of Gramsci (1971) and Freire (1972), states that this alternative, collective political education approach 'should be based upon active community participation and empowerment . . . and the *transformation* of economic, social and political (including personal) and cultural relations in society' (1997, p.22). This educational approach is referred to as training for transformation.

The role of the worker in community learning

Forrester identifies that education does not take place without the facilitation of a worker. He states that 'citizenship activity and learning is unlikely to happen spontaneously' (2004, p.34). Mayo (1997) also sees a key role for the worker if alternative approaches to education are to be carried out. She states:

> the oppressed and exploited . . . need educators committed to processes of dialogue, between theoretical learning and experiential learning, between theory and reflective practice. And they need a critical understanding of the inter-relationships between ideological struggles, and material, economic, social, political and cultural struggles for transformation. (1997, p.30)

Mayo developed a model for locating the role of the educator and education programmes, which is useful to locate the work of Youth and Community Workers as informal educators.

Table 8.1 Contemporary approaches to adult education in various contexts (adapted from Mayo, 1997, p.58)

	Cut off from life	Integrated with life
	Tendency 1	**Tendency 2**
Not aimed at changing the socio-cultural and politico-economic environment	Academic/individualistic (non-vocational/practical)	Market led/training community based Fitting learners to markets
	Tendency 3	**Tendency 4**
Aimed at changing the socio-cultural and politico-economic environment	Professional and individualistic approaches Leader/professional worker as change agent	Collective approaches/ empowerment Education for transformation

Mayo's (1997) notions of 'cut off from life' and 'integrated with life' are similar to Putnam's (2000) notions of 'doing for' (cut off) communities and 'doing with' (integrated), or being part of a community and working alongside others. In Tendency 1 and 3, the educational process is individualized and may be led by an external professional. In Tendencies 2 and 4 work is within the community, community based and collective. The table also locates the possible role of the educator if any. The individualized volunteering approaches mentioned in Chapter 4, which mainly generate human capital, can be located in Tendency 1. There is potentially little role for the informal educator in this tendency. Active citizenship, if working to a preset curriculum and doing the work of the state, could be located in Tendency 2. The role of the professional Youth and Community Worker could be seen to be located in Tendency 3.

Critical, collective community learning, such as that of the Active Learning for Active Citizenship pilots, would fall within Tendency 4, and has an important role in the enabling of social capital, a prerequisite of community engagement, citizenship and civil and civic involvement.

Education can be seen to be an important element and prerequisite for citizenship, both individual and collective. This table shows that the type of education can influence the citizenship action and as a result determine whether it produces social, human or state capital. Conversely, the types of capital are recognized as having differing impacts on education, for example the processes involved in the production of social capital enhances education and 'social connectedness boosts educational attainment' (Putnam, 2000, p.306).

A template for enabling community learning

Drawing on the discussion above it is possible to provide a template to use when planning and implementing community learning using informal education.

The template uses the key characteristics of Freirian popular education, linked to the cycle of reflective critical practice (as discussed in Chapter 9), set in a community of practice . . . a space within a community. It is also realistic, incorporating the requirements of current practice to show outcomes and outputs. Evaluation is assisted by including an initial stage where starting points or base lines are identified and agreed.

Most importantly, at the outset, and as a prerequisite for practice, you must locate your practice. This should ensure that your work is not dominated by the constraints of social policy or funding requirements. This has to be done in relation to the principles and approaches of Youth and Community Work (for example as set out in the NYA Ethical Statement for Youth Work, see Chapter 9) and also taking into account your own perspective and identity. For example a woman worker using a feminist perspective would carry out women's work very differently from a male worker using a New Right perspective!

As with all Youth and Community Work your involvement has to be negotiated and the participants have to engage voluntarily. Your role is to support and enrich what may be already existing groups and activities, and to help identify and facilitate new areas for action.

ACTIVITY **8.2**

Consider an actual informal education process of community learning that you have been or are involved with, or one that you think has the potential to take place. Fill in the second column showing how you are involved and what takes place though the whole of the learning process.

ACTIVITY 8.2 *continued*

Template for enabling community learning

Worker's role	Evidence of group active learning process
Prerequisite. Locate yourself and your practice. Be aware of own and professional identity, perspective, and strengths.	
1. Engage with an existing group or develop a group! Negotiate, and agree your involvement.	
2. Create a safe, inclusive space (undertake preparation including ethical considerations).	
3. Discuss, drawing on participants' experience (choose relevant topics). Agree a base line starting point.	
4. Become aware of issues/requirements.	
5. Identify area/s for exploration (problem pose).	
6. Debate, deliberation, dialogue, ask 'why' questions?	
7. Analyse at a personal, cultural and societal (PCS) level.	
8. Identify areas for action at PCS level.	
9. Identify areas for training and support, (e.g. skills and knowledge required by group and worker).	
10. Support change/transformation.	
11. Evaluation/reflection (by the group and worker), identify outcomes, and repeat the process!	

The table clarifies the worker's role in enabling the informal education process. It may also be possible for groups to move through this process without the facilitation of a worker, depending on their levels of confidence and group functioning. Consciousness raising groups such as men's groups, women's groups and peer education projects will have a different role for any Youth and Community Worker involvement. In these cases any worker involvement might be in the form of an ally, for example providing information, support, training and resources if requested.

Using the template above, the role of the worker would be to enable the group to start with an issue of importance or relevance to them and work through discussions of how this situation impacts on them, and look for similarities and patterns with other communities and contexts. This can then be discussed at a community, society and global level. In the same way the possible explanations should be discussed at local, societal and global levels, and action be identified in these areas. For example, an asylum seeker who was part of a refugee and migrant worker forum, and could not get access to health care, recognized this was a shared experience with others in a similar situation. The group discussed the impact on them, their family and community, and discussed the cause of this situation. It was not the fault of the individual but a result of the local interpretation of national regulations, which were in response to a global situation. The group decided to take action at a local level by writing to their local primary care trust, and raised a petition which was taken to their Member of Parliament and the House of Commons.

Using the PCS model discussed in Chapters 6 and 7 work with groups should help the worker to understand the socio-political, economic and structural causes of inequality and exclusion and so help prevent pathologizing, or blaming the individual. It should also enable us as individuals to see that we all have an important part to play in making change that will ripple out from our actions, with cumulative effect, as individuals and as members of groups and communities.

Recognizing and acknowledging learning and achievement

Outcomes and outputs from community learning

As identified in the template for enabling community learning, the identification and measurement of outcomes and outputs is an increasing requirement of our work.

As Youth and Community Workers have a facilitating and enabling role, our contributions are not always apparent and the outcomes of what have been achieved are often unrecognized and unrecorded. Much of the work that takes place is developmental and capacity building at an individual, group and organizational level. The ALAC pilots showed those who were involved had to get better at identifying what was being achieved and the impacts that were being made not only at the personal level (for example, Jay has now obtained employment) but also at the civic (democratic) and civil (society) levels. For this to happen we have to become better at recognizing, valuing and setting the type of indicators of community engagement and active citizenship that are all too often seen as 'soft' and immeasurable. An example of this is given in Chapter 3 on civic and civil engagement, which draws on the ALAC/Take Part learning frameworks outcomes table (see www.takepart.org.uk).

ACTIVITY **8.3**

Access the Take Part learning framework section 1.8, 'The outcomes of active citizenship' (p.24). Read the illustrations of learning and citizenship outcomes at a personal, community, civil and civic level.

ACTIVITY *8.3* *continued*

Draw a table showing these four types of outcomes. Identify a group that you have been working with. It could be the same group as discussed in the above exercise, and using the table identify the outcomes that are being gained by the participants in the group.

Recognizing achievements

When you have reached a point in an educational process where evaluation has taken place and outcomes recognized you should consider if you want to recognize what has been achieved in some way. There is a variety of ways to recognize achievements whether through celebratory events, sharing achievements with others at an individual, community and national level, or by certification. Celebration events are valuable to publicize the work undertaken by the group and any action that is being taken. For example, a group of women survivors of domestic abuse planned a conference, 'End the fear', for service providers in Manchester to publicize the findings of their research regarding accessibility to health services for women experiencing domestic abuse. The conference also included time for the presentation of certificates for the research team, and a discussion of the methods used that gave them a voice and control over the content of the work.

Accreditation and progression

It is possible to link the work that you are carrying out with groups into accreditation bodies that will give recognition to the learning and achievements of the participants. Some organizations such as that of the Open College Network (OCN) will give accreditation for a course that can be designed and delivered by the community group (for an overview of a range of possible courses and accrediting bodies see the Take Part learning framework section 2.5, 'Progression route', (p.45) www.takepart.org/framework-for-active-learning).

At an individual level a five-step process known as RARPA (Recognizing and Recording Progress and Achievement) has been established and can be used with participants in community learning activities. The individual accreditation requires that the individual identifies that they want to take part in the RARPA process at the start of the activity. Their process through the five stages can be assisted by a worker or peer from within the group (the five steps being, identifying the aim and the purpose of their work, identifying their existing skills and knowledge, identifying what they want to learn, and how they are going to do this, identifying how this will be recognized and recorded, and finally recognizing the learning that has taken place). This process has been developed by NIACE and the Learning and Skills Development Agency (LSDA), and is recognized by the Learning and Skills Council. RARPA can be used by any organization delivering non-accredited learning and has been endorsed by the Qualifications and Curriculum Authority (QCA) (see www.qca.org.uk).

Individuals who wish to gain a qualification following an individual portfolio route can also complete the City and Guilds Individual Profile in Active Citizenship. It uses a 'distance-travelled' model, allowing for personal choice when selecting from the wide range of citizenship activities.

To explore some of the different citizenship qualifications that are available, you can go to the QCA's website at: www.openquals.org.uk/openquals. This enables you to search for details of qualifications and exam boards by using a keyword search engine (www.takepart.org).

In other cases it is possible to undertake modules that are run from further or higher education programmes. Some of these may be 'first steps' or taster modules; others may be part of existing programmes. The case study below illustrates the application of such accredited modules from Manchester Metropolitan University.

It is important that the content of any learning should suit the requirements and direction of the group, not vice versa. The programme should be flexible enough to enable the participants and the trainer/facilitator to adapt them to the requirements, interests and experience of each group. Any accreditation and the level of courses should not be a barrier to participation, either in relation to selection by ability or by adding perceived formality or pressure, or to restrict the capacity and remit of the organic activists who are involved.

The challenge of the programmes that have sought to offer recognition and the potential of progression within education has been to provide the benefits and rigours of accreditation without perpetuating the constraints of formal education which might have stifled the potential for transformation and change, which is inherent in formal education.

CASE STUDY

The Community Audit and Evaluation Centre at Manchester Metropolitan University has been delivering a range of community based accredited courses, some co-designed with community partners, all co-delivered with partners. The MMU accredited participatory research and evaluation Community Audit module consists of ten two hour sessions delivered along side the community based team carrying out research or evaluations. The content of the module plus the activity involves working with groups through the three stages of the process of preparation, gathering information, and then analysing, report writing and dissemination. Sessions are a combination of theory and practice. During the programme, the groups explore principles, methodologies and appropriate methods and information gathering techniques, ethics and issues of inclusion, exclusion and repre-sentation and predicting and avoiding blocks and barriers, and planning and evaluating. The programmes have involved groups such as Groundwork, which hosted a team of community volunteers in Tameside to research the requirements for effective volunteering. In Manchester three teams, two of women and one from minority ethnic communities, have been researching the barriers to employment for those from marginalized communities. The South Manchester Healthy Living Network's (HLN) programme involved the recruitment of a group of volunteers from a team already working as volunteers and peer health educators. The findings of the evaluation resulted in recommendations for the effective support of the HLN's Discovery Team of volunteers, plus a separate report for the HLN with recommendations for effective working with community groups.

Progression

Although accreditation from further and higher education can be used for credits for progression to further study, progression should not only refer to educational developments. Progression achieved by the participants can also be in relation to personal growth, community engagement and the impact on civic and civil life.

As identified by Jill Bedford and Sue Gorbing, the facilitators from the West Midlands ALAC hub,

> *Accreditation is always viewed as an option, and for some women formal OCN accreditation is not important. One woman did not choose to gain OCN recognition but instead enrolled directly onto a Foundation Degree. For others, progression is to do with becoming more confident and more active in community and public life.*

Conclusion

This chapter has discussed the characteristics of informal education as a community learning process, to enable you as a Youth and Community Worker to have a greater understanding of your role in enabling active community based learning. You will have a greater understanding of the requirements for effective learning, and strategies to undertake and facilitate experiential learning.

Although individual learning can take place through reflective practice for workers and participants alike, the importance of groups as social environments for learning is emphasized. The process of informal education with such groups is identified and types of community learning and their outcomes and various ways of recognizing achievement indicated.

Enabling learning environments and processes is an essential tool for Youth and Community Workers, particularly those involved in supporting active citizenship type activities in communities. As David Blunkett, the initiator of the Active Learning for Active Citizenship programme, stated: 'it is not just about better outcomes, crucial though they are. It is also about what happens to communities along the way, what they learn about themselves and each other, the way they develop and grow' (HO, 2003, p.1).

REFERENCES

Banks, S, Butcher, H, Henderson, P and Robertson, J, eds (2003) *Managing community practice*. Bristol: Policy Press.

Butcher, H, Banks, S, Henderson, P and Robertson, J eds (2007*) Critical community practice*. Bristol: Policy Press.

Department of Communities and Local Government (DCLG) (2006) *The community development challenge*. West Yorkshire: Communities and Local Government.

Forrester, K (2004) *Towards democratic citizenship through non-formal education. Final project report*. Dublin: Tallaght Partnership.

Freire, P (1972) *Pedagogy of the oppressed*. London: Penguin Books.

Gramsci, A. (1971) *Selections from the prison notebooks*. London: Lawrence and Wishart.

Gilchrist, A. (2001) Working with networks and organizations in the community, in LD Richardson, M Wolfe, eds, *Principles and practice of informal education*. London: RoutledgeFalmer.

Home Office (HO), (Blunkett, D) (2003) *Active citizens, strong communities – progressing civil renewal*. London: Home Office.

Ledwith, M (1997) *Participating in transformation: Towards a working model of community empowerment*. Birmingham: Venture Press.

Ledwith, M (2006) *Community development: A critical approach*. Bristol: Policy Press.

Life Long Learning UK (LLLUK) (2008) Common standards for community learning and development. London: Sector Skills Development Agency/LLUK.

Mayo, M (1997) *Imagining tomorrow. Adult education for transformation*. Leicester: NIACE.

Putnam, RD (2000) *Bowling alone: The collapse and revival of American community*. New York: Simon and Schuster.

Popple, K (2000) *Analysing community work*. Buckingham: Open University Press.

Richardson, LD and Wolfe, M (2001) *Principles and practice of informal education*. London: RoutledgeFalmer.

Twelvetrees, A (2002) *Community work*. Basinstoke: Palgrave.

Wenger, E (2005) A social theory of learning, in R Harrison and C Wise, eds, *Working with young people*. London: The Open University Press/Sage, pp.142–149.

Woodward, V (2004) *Active learning for active citizenship*. London: Home Office.

Woodward, V (2008) Reflections on active learning for active citizenship, in J Annette and M Mayo, eds, *Active learning for active citizenship?* Leicester: NIACE.

WEBSITES

www.lifelonglearninguk.org

Chapter 9
The effective practitioner

This chapter outlines the processes of effective practice. This includes using reflection, being aware of the factors to consider when making a judgement, and considering a range of possible strategies for action. Reflection is discussed as not merely being retrospective, but also as a process of critical analysis and evaluation that should take place in the present, and with regard to future planning. The processes discussed to enable effective practice are advocated for use not only by Youth and Community Workers, but also as part of the implementation of informal education and community learning for participants.

ACTIVITY **9.1**

Identify a situation or incident that you were directly involved with, preferably in your role as a Youth and Community Worker. You may have thought it positive or it may have had a negative outcome. Record what took place and the actions that you took, if any, as a result of the incident. Your recording will be the basis for another task at the end of the chapter.

Reflective practice is part of the process of ongoing learning and development for both the worker and participant and will enhance the opportunity for what we do to be more effective. The discussions in this book have been part of a process of reflective practice. To be able to write this, I have gone through a process of drawing on my own and other people's experiences. I have also drawn on theories, ideas and principles and drawn up some models to help in the process of contextualizing and critiquing our practice to enable us to be more effective workers. The process of critical reflective practice involves the linking of theory and ideas to practice, what Paulo Freire referred to as praxis, drawing on what Schön (1983) calls a repertoire of information and skills to enable us to make better informed judgements, leading to effective decisions and actions.

In this book I have discussed the process of informal education within Youth and Community Work, drawing on the popular education theory of Paulo Freire (1972). I have discussed the issues involved in community involvement with civil and civic engagement, and the production of human, social and state capital drawing on the work of Putnam (2000) in particular considering what or who benefits from activity. I have discussed the complexity of work with volunteers and critiqued the notions of novice and expert. I have made the case that roles are context and task specific. It is intended that these models, frameworks and theories can help in the process of reflecting on practice.

For example, taking into consideration the volunteer type framework (Table 4.2, p.48) will mean that new volunteers are not all expected to be inexperienced or lacking in knowledge. This knowledge can affect how you work with a volunteer or community activist, who may not be able to use the photocopier but knows a great deal about the needs of their local community!

However, the range of factors that need to be drawn on are themselves not sufficient for effective practice. Effective reflective practice requires critical analysis and the application of a political framework, such as the feminist framework advocated by Kerry Young (2008). For example, we can work with girls in 'girls only' groups in ways that might reinforce gender stereotypes (e.g. hair and beauty sessions) or we can carry out girls' work using a feminist perspective, which would critique labelling and discuss identity and empowerment. Butcher et al. (2007) see this process as an essential requirement for 'critical community practice' which requires 'critical consciousness'.

Critical consciousness is based upon theoretical assumptions regarding the importance of human interaction, communication and group formation and function, particularly the ability for discussion and democratic decision making. These assumptions are coupled with a commitment to social justice, social inclusion, social self determination and social solidarity (Butcher et al., 2007).

The processes of Freirian popular education discussed in Chapter 2, leading from problem posing to action, can therefore be taken at an individual worker level as well as part of a group process. Ledwith (2005) draws on the Frierian characteristics of popular education as the basis for a model of critical praxis and a critical approach to community development. She advocates that it is essential to understand and locate the internal and external forces in a community and how they impact and cause oppression, so that you can 'develop a framework within which smaller projects can be seen as contributing to a bigger whole. Otherwise, community workers can be either sucked into impotence and despair or respond with palliatives that are incoherent in the long term quest for social justice' (Ledwith, 2005, p.40).

This chapter will outline the development of this critical reflective process.

The development of reflective effective practice in Youth and Community Work education and training

Youth and Community Work courses are different from those in more formal educational sectors, which may take on a more didactic approach and be committed to the passing on of a collection of knowledge by an expert. In Youth and Community Work training and education those that facilitate learning apply the informal education and popular education principles that have been discussed in this book. Although, like all workers, we are constrained by the restrictions and expectations of our institution we are able to apply the principles and methods of informal education within our courses. To do otherwise would be hypocritical and counter-productive.

Within our courses students are expected to show development of themselves as practitioners and in relation to knowledge and awareness. What is expected is set out in course documents for each of the different levels, e.g. what students are expected to demonstrate in assignments and in practice tasks, and for the different grades given. At the start of the programme it is expected that you are able to show that you have an understanding of the key issues that are basic to our profession, coupled with an awareness of your self as a practitioner. This awareness is essential if you are to recognize the skills and knowledge required to undertake your role, and also be able to understand how who you are impacts on your work and those around you. Increasingly you will be expected to show that you have a wider understanding of yourself and those you work with in a broader context. This is similar to the PCS model used by Thompson (1998/2005) to discuss dealing with discrimination. Awareness and action are needed at a personal, cultural and societal/structural level. You should be able to consider the impact of immediate situations but also see the effect of wider community, societal and global issues. This critical perspective does not focus solely on the individual and their immediate needs, but looks at the cause of situations and considers 'why'. Illustrations of this have been given elsewhere in this book, for example in the section on the Schools of Participation in Chapter 6 on enabling participation.

Added to this, it is expected that you should be able to show a critical awareness and be able to critique information and experiences. This process means that you do not merely understand what other people have said but that you can analyse and locate ideas, for example in undertaking a particular perspective. I have advocated in this book that we adopt a critical perspective. Others do not share this view and do not give weight to an approach that considers the impact of power and powerlessness, prejudice and discrimination. Rather, they may focus on biologically determined factors (e.g. people are poor, unequal or 'bad' because it is genetically inherited), or the rights of the individual in a free market economy (e.g. you get what you earn or can buy).

The importance of being able to be an aware, reflective and critical practitioner is that you will become a more effective practitioner. The components of this are discussed below. They include being aware of our accountability, which entails applying the ethics that underpin our practice, using the process of critical reflection prior, during and after action, and importantly making well informed decisions and taking effective action.

Effective practice

The importance of being more aware of what we do is so that we can be more efficient and effective in our role. Youth and Community Workers cannot rely on physical technical tools as a surgeon or carpenter would. In most situations we are the only and most important resource that we will have. We therefore have to make sure that we are working as effectively as possible. To enable us to develop our effectiveness we need to be aware of to whom we are accountable.

Accountability

Accountability is a concept that originates in financial checking. It draws on the practice of being called on to give an account of what you have done or have not done (Banks, 2002). In the case of Youth and Community Workers, accountability is a complex process caused by the different people and groups that a worker may be accountable to.

ACTIVITY 9.2

As a worker for a small voluntary organization you have been involved with a group of local volunteers organizing a community festival. You have received some local authority funding and income from local businesses and the community through donations. Who do you consider needs feedback on the event, and why?

This example has used financial checking as one element of accountability. This is not the only area where people should receive feedback. In the above example the people who have contributed to the festival in a variety of ways should be told how that contribution has been used and to what effect. For example the number of people who attended and their composition may be the result of good and varied publicity. The fact that few injuries were reported to the Red Cross first-aiders will be a result of good stewarding and health and safety checks. The amount raised through the raffle is the result of a good gate volunteers' rota. All of this may have been carried out by volunteers who will want their contribution to have been effective and recognized. A new festival coordinator recruited from the local community may have been supported by you and others to undertake the work for the first time. In addition to these areas, funders will also want to know how their money has been spent and what has been achieved.

Using this example it can be seen that Youth and Community Workers are therefore accountable to:

1. employers, funders and commissioners of services;

2. service users or participants engaged with our practice (the public/community);

3. our profession and community of practice;

4. ourselves.

The complexity of this means that there are likely to be conflicts of interest or dilemmas as to whom we are most accountable to, and at times we will have complex or multiple accountabilities (Banks, 2002). This is evident in the statement of principles of ethical conduct for youth work which recognizes that 'these accountabilities may be in conflict' (NYA, 2004, p.6). Banks argues that accountability and a preparedness to lay 'oneself open to criticism' to those diverse interests to whom we are accountable, presents youth workers 'with their most acute dilemmas about what constitutes ethical practice' (Banks, 2002, p.37).

Accountability to employers

For many workers they would consider that they are first and foremost accountable to their managers or their 'boss', for example 'through hierarchical organizational power structures or contract compliance' (Barr, 2003, p.137). This may require the keeping of administrative records in relation to incidents, attendance or outcomes gained, and regular reporting on work undertaken.

Within voluntary and community organizations this will not only mean reporting to a line manager or team leader, but may also mean reporting to a management committee, who are legally the worker's employer. This group of people, who will all be volunteers, will be legally responsible for the financial accounting of the organization, and the well being and safety of their employees and service users.

Commissioning procedures, where local authorities contract other organizations to carry out work on their behalf, will expect someone representing the voluntary organization to formally agree that they meet the legal obligations of Acts dealing with health and safety, food hygiene, race relations, child protection, and disability discrimination. The worker has to ensure that they work within these guidelines and frameworks on behalf of the organization, being directly accountable to their line manager. The plethora of legal requirements of workers and organizations, mean that accountability to our employer can dominate our practice.

Management accountability

The area of accountability which increasingly causes most dilemmas on a day-to-day basis is that of management accountability. You will have the chance to consider these issues using the case studies below. For example, you may be employed by an organization, but your wages may be funded through several sources, and you work as part of a multi-agency team, all of whom may want you to be accountable to them in relation to outcomes and outputs.

Accountability to service users

We also are accountable to those with whom we work, the service users or participants. As has been discussed in earlier chapters, government policies such as best value, local authority compact agreements with the community and voluntary sectors, the White Paper on Strong and Prosperous Communities (2006), and the 'Together We Can' strategy (DCLG ongoing) have increasingly built in an obligation for the engagement of service users and communities in the identification of local needs and in the delivery of services. As a result, service users are increasingly viewed as 'stakeholders with a crucial contribution to make to performance measurement' (Barr, 2003, p.137). This has led to the concept of mutual accountability and a partnership between the 'governors and governed' (Barr, 2003, p.152). Workers are clearly now accountable to the public, and the consequence of new government initiatives may be that these community stakeholders become increasingly accountable for the decisions and actions they are jointly involved with.

We should also involve service users in identifying and agreeing areas for work. Participants in activities are often asked to draw up guidelines for behaviour and what they hope to achieve from their involvement. These practices mean that the members of the group then also be come accountable to each other for their actions.

Accountability to the Youth and Community Work profession

Our accountability to our profession is of central importance, and in a time of multi-agency working is essential to enable us to work across professional boundaries, keeping sight of our professional contribution and stance. Reference to this can be through the principles and vision statements of Youth and Community Work and importantly via our ethical statements.

The ethics of our practice can be summarized drawing on the ethical principles of medical practice. We should

- do our best to do good, so enhance well being;
- do no harm;
- enable and respect the autonomy and rights of the individual;
- seek to be fair.

These basic elements are evident in most ethical statements and can be identified in the Ethical Statement for Youth Work shown here.

National Youth Agency, Ethical Conduct in Youth Work

1.1. The purpose of youth work is to facilitate and support young people's growth through dependence to interdependence, by encouraging their personal and social development and enabling them to have a voice, influence and place in their communities and society.

1.2. Youth work is informed by a set of beliefs which includes a commitment to equal opportunity, to young people as partners in learning and decision-making and to helping young people to develop their own sets of values. We recognize youth work by these qualities:

- it offers its services in places where young people can choose to participate;
- it encourages young people to be critical in their responses to their own experience and to the world around them;
- it works with young people to help them make informed choices about their personal responsibilities within their communities;
- it works alongside school and college-based education to encourage young people to achieve and fulfil their potential; and
- it works with other agencies to encourage society to be responsive to young people's needs.

Summary of the statement of principles of ethical conduct for youth work

Ethical principles
Youth workers have a commitment to:

1. *Treat young people with respect, valuing each individual and avoiding negative discrimination.*

2. *Respect and promote young people's rights to make their own decisions and choices, unless the welfare or legitimate interests of themselves or others are seriously threatened.*

3. *Promote and ensure the welfare and safety of young people, while permitting them to learn through undertaking challenging educational activities.*

4. *Contribute towards the promotion of social justice for young people and in society generally, through encouraging respect for difference and diversity and challenging discrimination.*

Professional principles
Youth workers have a commitment to:

5. *Recognize the boundaries between personal and professional life and be aware of the need to balance a caring and supportive relationship with young people with appropriate professional distance.*

6. *Recognize the need to be accountable to young people, their parents or guardians, colleagues, funders, wider society and others with a relevant interest in the work, and that these accountabilities may be in conflict.*

7. *Develop and maintain the required skills and competence to do the job.*

8. *Work for conditions in employing agencies where these principles are discussed, evaluated and upheld.*

(National Youth Agency, 2004).

Self accountability

In relation to ourselves, this refers to our own value base which may be informed by religious or political beliefs and might at times come into conflict with what we are asked to carry out for our work. In situations where our beliefs may mean that we cannot meet the requirements of our job description then we may no longer be able to carry on with that work. (In this case we would have placed our personal accountability above that to our profession or employers.)

We also have to engage in a process of 'critical self awareness and reflexivity' (Banks, 2007, p.140) or critical reflection, where the dimension of political analysis and the recognition of the influence of values and perspectives are included.

The aim of reflective practice is to be more aware of factors such as the impact of multiple accountabilities, to enable us to make better informed judgements and be more effective practitioners.

Using reflection to aid effective practice

The ability to analyse our practice critically is an essential skill for Youth and Community Workers. This is aided by the process referred to as reflective practice. However, as will be discussed here, this is not purely a process of looking back. It can also be carried out whilst undergoing action in the present, and when preparing for activity in the future. All three types of reflection will require you to draw on a repertoire of skills, and knowledge, drawn from theory, models of practice and ethical principles.

Reflection as looking back, analyses and evaluates what has taken place. This is also sometimes referred to as illuminative evaluation, where the process of looking back can 'shed light' on something, looking at the whole situation in a subjective way with the purpose of informing future practice as opposed to more rigid, inspectoral types of evaluation. This process was called by Donald Schön (1930–1997) 'reflection-on-action'. This process involves a thorough analysis of who was involved, what took place, where, when, how and 'importantly' an attempt to understand why. This analysis would then lead to an evaluation with suggestions made for future action.

Reflection whilst you are involved in an activity was referred to by Schön as 'reflection-in-action' where what you have learnt is put into practice through a process of conscious competence or 'thinking on our feet . . ., It involves looking to our experiences, connecting with our feelings, and attending to our theories in use. It entails building new understandings to inform our actions in the situation that is unfolding' (Smith, 2007, np).

Schön's work indicated that learning did not need to go through a whole process of a learning cycle such as that identified by Kolb or Dewey, but that learning could take place by the application of the repertoire of skills and knowledge in the present.

In addition to analysing what you have done, drawing on that to enable effective practice in the present, Thompson (2005) adds to Schön's categories of reflection that of 'reflection-before-action', what I call the process of 'predict, plan and prevent'. That is the process of gathering together all the information you may have to help you make an informed decision. The process of making effective decisions is outlined below.

The aim of reflective practice should be that we move through a process of *unconscious incompetence*, where we are not aware of our actions, through *conscious incompetence*, where we are made aware that our practice, knowledge or awareness needs to be developed, to the state of *conscious competence*, where reflection in action may take place. This may result in the state of *unconscious competence*, where we have reached a level of experience and good practice that does not warrant continuous introspection.

The ability to use reflection to improve on your practice has been placed on a spectrum by Knott and Scragg (2007), who suggest a hierarchy of reflection. They state that the

novice is characterized by adherence to taught rules with little discretionary judgement while the expert is characterized by freedom from rules and guidelines with an intuitive grasp of situations, based on deep understanding, knowing what is possible, using analytical approaches in novel situations or when a new problem occurs. Thus the expert stage is characterized by implicitly and unconscious practice. (2007, p.8)

This would indicate an element of self awareness, and the types of competence outlined above have similarities to the areas of the Johari Window model (Luft, 1969). Here the dynamics of what is known to you and what is known to others about you are joined through the process of being able to give and receive feedback, so that the arena of known to self and known to others is expanded. In team work this is viewed as the most productive area for the group where there is good communication.

However, it is likely that Thompson and others who adopt a critical perspective of practice would argue that, although a certain element of competence or expertise is desirable, our work should always be consciously considered, for example, being aware of the context or socio-political situation in which our practice is taking place.

This would mean that we are involved in an ongoing process of praxis linking theory and practice, recognizing that the resulting potential for change will be affected by dimensions of power and difference that have to be continually acted upon and challenged.

The characteristics of reflective practice can be seen as being that it

- is a political process, affected by power dynamics;
- occurs within a social context;
- is shaped by ideology and history;
- is action oriented;
- involves enquiry;
- requires deconstruction of practice;
- requires reconstruction of meaning; and
- is problem posing and problem solving.

(drawn from Day, 1993)

The elements of this reflective practice process have been central to the discussion of informal education discussed in this book. The informal education approach forms an essential element of the link between theory and practice (praxis). It is based on problem posing, critical dialogue and awareness raising or conscientization. It has a focus on action and transformation/change and a commitment to social justice. It is therefore an essential component of the learning process for the worker and participants.

Being an effective practitioner does not solely mean analysing practice and incidents, but the worker must also draw on the range of factors discussed here to make a judgement about action in the present and future.

To enable you to make effective judgements and be an effective reflective practitioner you can engage in what Schön called single or double loop learning. If you are involved in single loop learning, the process, although valuable, is restricted and limited as there is no involvement of others to help in the critiquing or introspection of your actions.

> *Single loop learning = planning, delivery and evaluation, done in private, so disempowering growth.*

> *Double loop learning = planning, delivery and evaluation are an explicit and accessible process, personal theories are examined and made public.*

Similar to the informal education process, double loop learning involves the worker in a space for critical dialogue and reflection on action and experience with others.

Making a judgement involves drawing on:

- *accountability (e.g. service users, profession, agency, self);*
- *reflection on your previous experience;*
- *context (who, where, how);*
- *legal requirements (e.g. policy);*
- *agreements (group, organizational and individual contracts);*
- *ethics;*
- *values;*
- *principles;*
- *power and difference;*
- *own agency (e.g. self confidence, identity);*
- *history;*
- *predicting possible outcomes;*
- *theory (bodies of ideas that can inform our actions).*

Intervention should be based on a conscious process, making a judgement based on all the factors above.

Reflective practice case studies

CASE STUDY

1. A service user you are working with comes into your centre wearing a new jacket. It is apparent that it is new as the label is evident on the sleeve. You believe that the coat is stolen.

CASE STUDY

2. A service user comes to your agency evidently under the influence of alcohol or some other drug. They are acting very oddly and you feel they are dangerous.

CASE STUDY

3. You are working as part of a team drawn from different agencies on a project to deliver services to young people. One of the lead agencies had made a decision without your agreement.

Drawing on the list of considerations for making a judgement, what factors would you consider before taking action in each of the case studies above?

Helping reflective practice

On an individual level we can aid the process of any of the three types of reflective practice (reflection on, in or before action) in a variety of ways.

Recordings and a reflective diary such as those required for a learning development portfolio are an effective way of enabling analysis and evaluation.

There are some legal or managerial requirements for particular types of recordings such as incident recordings, for example, where there has been a racist incident, or for health and safety reasons if someone has had an accident. These tend to be fairly factual. These may help with reflective practice by an analysis of what took place is required and may assist with future prevention. However, to meet the requirement of effective reflective practice, analytical recordings need to take into account a broader analysis of what took place, including self reflection by the workers involved.

We can actively seek to draw on evidence and information to **inform** our practice, for example what others have said through research, theory or writing.

We must be **well informed** in relation to policies, requirements and procedures that frame our work.

We can make the most of **others** and supervision, or discussion opportunities, perhaps by preparing notes and queries.

We must seek to be **self aware** of our learning styles and who we are and how we impact on others and our practice.

We should follow Youth and Community Work **principles and ethics** as set out in the table (on pp.124–5) making sure that we are aware of the **impact of power and difference** on our practice and the potential for participation of service users.

We can learn from new **experiences** either directly or vicariously through a variety of media. This is the rationale for the practice placements and the requirement that both the placements must be in different settings.

We also have to be prepared to **give and receive feedback**, and to listen effectively.

If the more productive double loop reflection is to take place, then analysis and evaluation should take place with others. This can be done by being part of a group, through team meetings, working with a mentor or tutor, and supervision. Recordings can be used as the basis for discussion and deliberation. Here the process of critical dialogue and the giving and receiving of feedback can aid in learning and so improve practice. This can be done virtually through electronic discussion forums as well as through face to face conversations.

The process of learning collaboratively, working with others in a critical community, is part of what is termed the co-production of knowledge. This approach is now increasingly highly regarded as a way of generating information, rather than that solely based on information from those who have been termed experts.

For both individual and collective reflective practice to take place the creation of space is essential, whether this be in relation to time for thinking and recording or, importantly, to engage in critical conversations and deliberations.

Using reflective practice as part of critical Youth and Community Work practice

The process of analysing and evaluating your practice, learning and taking that learning forward into practice, using the abilities and knowledge acquired to improve on practice so that it becomes more intuitive, enabling you to plan for more effective interventions, has to be set in a context of using a critical perspective.

Brechin (2000, p.26) suggests that there are three elements of the critical practitioner:

- firstly, that you must be aware of the contexts in which actions take place;

- secondly, that you must set your practice within a framework of your values, such as a social justice approach which challenges discrimination and exclusion, and which aims to empower;

- thirdly, that you should be involved in a process of continual critical enquiry and personal and professional development, striving for improvement.

These three elements of Brechin's critical practitioner are further developed into a four component practice model of 'critical community practice' by Butcher et al. (2007).

The first component is that of 'critical consciousness', which informs the value base for our work. This is the foundation for the other components of critical theorizing, critical action and critical reflection.

Thompson (1998) also makes the case that

> *good practice should be critically reflective practice . . . it is not enough simply to reflect upon practice, the reflection needs to be critical, in the sense of not taking existing social arrangement for granted, not making assumptions that can legitimate, reinforce or accentuate existing patterns of inequality. (1998, p.216)*

The requirement for the use of a critical perspective is discussed in Chapter 2.

Critical reflective practice in challenging times

Although this chapter has argued for the importance of reflective practice to enable effective intervention, it is increasingly viewed as being too loose and impossible to measure at a time when workers are increasingly being asked to quantify their work, set outcomes and outputs, and meet targets based on predetermined indicators.

This trend for providing evidence of what we do is based on an empirical, scientific approach, what Schön calls a technical/rational approach rather than the type of intuitive and emerging approach of reflective practice. The technical or evidence based approach can be incorporated into our practice if we draw on a range of evidence to validate our approaches and arguments. However, evidence based practice often sets predetermined expectations based on an already identified set of assumptions or theories. This is illustrated in many of the requirements of new funding streams which are often based on government identified priorities and desired outcomes. This is controlling and disempowering for the worker and the service user/participants. In such situations we, as Youth and Community Workers aiming to use informal education principles, arrive in a state of what Schön (1983) terms 'professional pluralism', where we have to find ways of 'functioning in situations of indeterminacy and value conflict'. As a result it may be impossible to analyse our practice using technical rationality, so Schön suggests that we use the art of 'reflection-in-action', through the process of 'knowing-in-practice'. This process of reflective practice has the potential to generate knowledge and ideas, and so to be a creative, empowering and transformative process for those involved.

CASE STUDY

The ALAC pilots

The debates between a proscribed process wanting recorded outcomes was evident in the Active Learning for Active Citizenship (ALAC) pilots carried out in seven areas across England between 2005 and 2007. The then Home Secretary had a clear idea that a set curriculum for

CASE STUDY *continued*

ALAC would entail particular elements that would meet the outcomes of the requirement for greater voluntary involvement with government priorities, such as engendering community cohesion, employability and policy formation. The ALAC pilots rejected the national curriculum approach as being too 'top down' and restrictive, and drew up a learning framework with principles and approaches (see Take Part, www.takepart.org). We were, however, still required to provide outcomes. These had not been preset, but were categorized to provide the evidence required for the Department of Communities and Local Government to show that our approach was working. These outcomes were in relation to individual, community civil and civic participation.

The outcomes as illustrated in the table below were identified at the end of the pilots by participants and facilitators, not set as indicators by an external expert (or the Home Office!) to be met and tested from the outset.

Examples of active citizenship outcomes (see the National Framework for ALAC, p.24, www.takepart.org/framework-for-active-learning)

Types of active citizenship	Learning outcomes	Citizenship outcomes
Personal	Value own skills knowledge and confidence. Know where to go to get what you need.	People take leadership roles in their community. People voice their concerns.
Community relations	Recognize that social exclusion is the responsibility of all and know what can do about it.	Community projects are inclusive of people from different backgrounds.
Civil participation	Know how to encourage it and democratic decision making.	Well run, democratic community groups.
Civic engagement	Recognize how to influence policy and practice at a European, national, regional or local level.	More people take part in dialogue with decision makers. People lobby for change to the way forums and other structures operate.

Taking action and dealing with dilemmas

The most important element of reflective and critical practice is making judgements that lead to effective action. As already discussed, there are contextual factors that need to be considered, coupled with complex accountability. There may rarely be a clear path of action. In some cases this will lead to an ethical dilemma. Banks (2003) states that an ethical dilemma will be evident if you have to make a choice between two equally unwelcome alternatives, and you may not be clear what the right one is. However, an ethical problem occurs if you feel that you are clear about your course of action but that there is something or someone preventing this. Many such ethical dilemmas and problems have been discussed in this book in relation to active citizenship, particularly with regard to the role of active citizens in the work of the state for civic as opposed to civil engagement and renewal.

In such situations short and long term benefits, as well as issues of accountability and ethics, have to be considered for all concerned.

Strategy options

To help understand the range of options and their consequences, a range of strategies are available for action. These are particularly useful to consider when dealing with a dilemma.

Option 1: Remain neutral, the implications are that you do nothing. However, it may not actually be possible to be truly impartial.

Option 2: State your commitment, and make known your views. This may be based on your principles or beliefs.

Option 3: Take a balanced approach, and consider and make known a wide range of alternative views, explanations and outcomes.

Option 4: Challenge consensus, or the dominant view, and take an oppositional view to that already being stated or held by the majority, or because you feel there is an alternative strong case.

(Adapted from Fiehn, 2005)

These strategy options are possible ways of dealing with situations or new information which may lead to a dilemma or a sense of unease, what Festinger (1957) called 'cognitive dissonance'. The situation recounted above in the ALAC pilots was one of cognitive dissonance, and what Schön called value conflict. The ALAC pilots decided on the option of challenging consensus, and through discussions with the Home Office representative and the ALAC steering group were able to make a case for the changing of the national ALAC approach.

Festinger suggested that in such a situation our options are to:

- Assimilate the information and whole-heartedly take it on board, absorbing it into our existing view or norms.

- Accommodate, so that we have to adapt our existing view in line with the new information or experience.

- Reject/ignore, if the new data or experience is thought to be too different or threatening so that it cannot be incorporated into our existing views or norms. This may mean that we do nothing.

- Challenge/fight, if the information is counter to our beliefs, norms or practices to the extent that we or a principle feel threatened, we may take action to challenge the view or behaviour.

- Distance/flight, in a situation where we feel powerless or overwhelmed, we may choose to remove ourselves from the dilemma or unease.

What we had done was to challenge the information we had been given based on a view that the Home Office approach to active citizenship was counter to our informal education principles.

ACTIVITY 9.3

The city council has decided to cut funding to your local community centre. This will most probably result in the closing of the centre and the loss of a base for many local groups, for example the Asian Women's Keep Fit group, a music group and Parent and Toddler group. The council has stated that they have concerns about the financial viability of the centre; local people believe the cut is the result of campaigning by the groups, which has been counter to the dominant political group. You have been asked to help take action to keep the centre open. You are employed by the city council.

Considering each of the options below what would be the strengths and weaknesses of each strategy? What would you do?

Stength	Stategy	Weakness
	Remain neutral	
	State commitment	
	Take a balanced approach	
	Challenge consensus	

The framework shows the range of alternative actions that may be used in any situation, particularly where we may experience a dilemma or ethical problem. As shown in the list of factors to consider, when making a judgement that leads to a course of action these actions have to be set in a context. For example, to do nothing does not mean that our actions are neutral and have no impact, we may be contributing to already existing power imbalances or perpetuating inequality and discrimination. For example, this would be the case if we did not challenge racist comments, and did not proactively plan to make sure our activities are inclusive. These strategies are discussed in more detail in Chapter 7 on inclusive and representative practice.

Reflective practice and community based learning and active citizenship

Much of the writing on the use of reflection in professional practice is with reference to the development and effective practice of the worker. However, the principles and approaches as set out here are central to community learning and active citizenship. Firstly, the experience of facilitating ALAC programmes has shown that there is a crucial facilitatory role for the worker to engage the participants in informal education in their own process of self reflection and transformation for change.

Secondly, this process of learning and the co-production of knowledge through critical engagement and reflection is enhanced by the participants working together in groups, such as those discussed here, for example in the Schools of Participation.

The worker should enable participants to analyse critically issues and situations, to draw on the range of factors to make informed decisions and be clear about the possible options for action and their consequences. Ideally, Youth and Community Workers might support community members to challenge the status quo if it was creating inequality and discrimination, as in the task above.

Conclusion

ACTIVITY **9.1** *revisited*

You should now look again at the initial recording activity you carried out at the start of the chapter. Considering the list of factors you should take into account when making a judgement. See if you would now make a different decision about the action you took. Also consider if you would have chosen a different strategy. Record any differences in your approach, the action taken, and why.

By discussing approaches to reflection and critical practice this chapter has provided a theoretical basis to assist you in locating and analysing your practice. Frameworks have been provided to enable you to make well informed and contextualized judgements and to see the range of strategies for intervention and their implications.

However, knowing what and how we should do this is not sufficient. As with the informal education practices outlined in this book, the most effective reflection and decision making about action are taken as part of a group or community where critical dialogue can take place. In addition, as with informal education, our considerations have to be set in a political context. To help us to carry out ongoing successful and effective reflective practice we therefore have to engage in critical conversation and engage with the 'broader social context' (Day, 1993, p.90) of our work. This not only necessitates the political location of our work but also that our work is open to public scrutiny, and critical analysis.

There are therefore several prerequisites to enable successful professional intervention:

1. We must have a clear sense of ourselves.

2. We have to consistently use the value base and ethical principles of Youth and Community Work.

3. We must utilize, and establish if necessary, a network of 'critical friends', or someone to provide supervision to enable conscious analytical reflection at the individual and social levels.

4. We should aim to establish, or work within, flexible organizational contexts which will enable and support reflective practice and its outcomes.

This chapter has therefore made the case that we must practise what we preach and apply informal education principles and practices, not only in the delivery of Youth and Community Work but in our own professional lives.

REFERENCES

Banks S, (2002) Professional values and accountabilities, in R Adams, L Dominelli and M Layne, eds, *Critical practice in social work*. Basingstoke: Palgrave, pp.28–37.

Banks, S (2003) Conflicts of culture and accountability: Managing ethical dilemmas and problems in community practice, in S Banks, H Butcher, P Henderson and J Robertson, eds, *Managing community practice*. Bristol: Policy Press, pp.103–120.

Banks, S (2007) Working in and with community groups and organizations: Processes and practices, in H Butcher, S Banks, P Henderson and J Robertson, eds, *Critical community practice*. Bristol: Policy Press, pp.77–96.

Barr, A (2003) Participative planning and evalution skills, in S Banks, H Butcher, P Henderson, P and J Robertson, eds. *Managing community practice*. Bristol: Policy Press, pp.137–153.

Batsleer, J (2008) Personal agendas, in *Reflective practice in the context of diversity in informal learning in youth work*. London: Sage.

Brechin, A (2000) Introducing critical practice, in A Brechin, H Brown and M Eby, eds, *Critical practice in health and social care*. London: Open University Press/Sage, pp. 25–47.

Butcher, H, Banks, S, Henderson, P and Robertson, J, eds (2007) *Critical community practice*. Bristol: Policy Press.

Day, C (1993) Reflection: A necessary but not sufficient condition for professional development. *British Educational Research Journal*, 19 (1): 83–93.

Festinger, L (1957) *Explorations in cognitive dissonance*. New York: Wiley.

Fiehn, J (2005) Agree to disagree, citizenship and controversial issues. London: DFES.

Freire, P (1972) *Pedagogy of the oppressed*. London: Penguin Books.

Knott, C and Scragg, T (2007) *Reflective practice in social work.* Exeter: Learning Matters.

Kolb, D (1984) *Experiential learning: Experience as the source of learning and development.* Englewood Cliffs, NJ: Prentice Hall.

Ledwith, M (2005) *Community development – a critical approach.* Bristol: BASW/Policy Press.

Luft, J (1969*) Of human interaction.* Palo Alto, CA: National Press.

National Youth Agency (2004) *Ethical conduct in youth work.* Leicester: NYA.

Putnam, R D (2000) *Bowling alone: The collapse and revival of American community*. New York: Simon and Schuster.

Schön, D (1983) *The reflective practitioner. How professionals think in action.* London: Temple Smith.

Smith, M (2007) Donald Schön: learning, reflection and change (www.Infed.org).

Thompson, N (1998) *Promoting equality.* Basingstoke: Macmillan.

Thompson, N (2005) *Understanding social work: Preparing for practice*. Basingstoke: Palgrave.

Thompson, N (2005) Anti-discriminatory practice, in R Harrison and C Wise, eds, *Working with young people*. London: Open University Press.

Young, K (2008) Has anything changed? Keynote speech at Feminist Webs Conference. Manchester: Manchester Metropolitan University.

Chapter 10
Taking the work forward

Reviewing the context

This book has drawn on work already being undertaken by Youth and Community Workers and has identified the areas that need to be in place, particularly those of participation and inclusion to enable informal education and community learning. Each chapter has set out key elements to enable us to be clearer about our role in relation to ethics and principles, and the changing demands of social policy and organizational constraints.

The timing of this book is crucial in relation to the growing emphasis on communities and active citizens. This may appear to be a golden opportunity for our work to be recognized and valued, or, alternatively, a means of 'doing us out of a job'. Government volunteering and active citizenship initiatives have placed the professional Youth and Community Worker in an identity crisis. The previous Conservative government's approach focused on the role of the individual in a free market economy denying the role of community, and individualizing concerns. During this period Youth and Community Work often adopted an oppositional position, working with communities and groups to tackle the structural causes of social exclusion. The stance of Youth and Community Workers, working with groups and individuals, in relation to and often counter to the state has been challenged by the New Labour government, which in addition to continuing the Conservative marketization has started to intervene into areas that were previously independent, particularly with regard community and voluntary organizations, and volunteers.

This is apparent by its desire to contract out previously state run services, and by introducing programmes to generate community cohesion and individual community engagement. The approach was first articulated by David Blunkett (HO, 2003), who was keen on the development of active citizens and their role in producing cohesive communities, but which has now been refined, giving a focus on civic engagement, governance and volunteering. This is reflected in the following statement from the Home Office Communities Group:

> communities are at the heart of the Government's agenda – the involvement of local people and voluntary, community and faith organizations is vital to bringing about real and sustained change across a wide range of important issues. These include tackling social exclusion, improving race equality and community cohesion, increasing volunteering and citizen engagement and supporting the voluntary and community sector to deliver more high quality public services. (HO, 2005, p.2)

Active citizenship is not a new concept for Youth and Community Workers. They have always worked to support self help activities and work with volunteers. However, we must critique whether the types of 'active citizenship' as promoted by such social policy initiatives engender social capital and the capacity for critical thinking and change, or are part of the generation of what I have called state and particularly punitive state capital.

We must consider if this is the continuation of New Right concepts developed as a replacement for social welfare and the responsibilities of the state, where 'the poorest in society are targeted to meet each other's needs' (Ledwith,1997, p.41). Here active citizenship is the 'charity-giving and community-serving caring face of capitalism' (p.41). In response, Ledwith calls for critical citizenship where workers and communities take collective responsibility for making structural changes.

A critical analysis of the role of voluntary involvement in relation to the state and society has been a theme throughout this book. The connectedness of community members through voluntary activity is seen as an important element of a vibrant and creative society. Prochaska states that

> *a decline in voluntary activity is a measure of decay within a liberal society. In the end, the political maturity of a country is . . . measured by a polity that provides the conditions of liberty conducive to civil society and by what citizens willingly do for themselves and one another. (2002, p.47)*

These views were echoed by Blunkett in *Active citizens, strong communities – progressing civil renewal*. He stated that John Dewey '. . . saw freedom as a value which can only be fully realized through positive engagement with the wider community' (HO, 2003, p.3).

More recently the government approach is evident in *Aiming high for young people: a ten year strategy for positive activities*. In the section entitled 'Building community cohesion' it states

> *work with young people is a critical starting point for tackling the tensions between different groups in the community. Positive activities, particularly through volunteering and inter-generational activities, can help to build better relations across the generations and between different groups of young people. (DfCSF, 2007, p.13)*

However, research by Annette and Creasy has shown that

> *Despite growing opportunities for participation through increased 'empowerment' in both national and local government, research suggests that people feel increasingly disconnected from the public realm . . . failure or reluctance to appreciate the 'political nature' of community leadership misses the opportunity to consider how involvement in neighbourhood renewal can give the opportunity for lifelong learning for active citizenship through partnership working . . . Which would benefit from being informed by the theory and practice of experiential learning . . .The main challenge facing such developments is whether local political authorities are willing and able to move beyond a politics of consumer satisfaction and public consultation to more deliberative and participatory democratic politics. (Annette and Creasy, 2007, pp.2–3)*

Annette and Creasy are therefore making a case for the facilitation of such experiential learning, what has been discussed in this book as informal education and community learning carried out by Youth and Community Workers.

The development of state capital

Government initiatives in relation to the community and its members are contradictory. One department encourages community empowerment and has developed 'An action plan for community empowerment' (DCLG, 2007b) identifying how local leaders, children and young people can be empowered, and how they can be involved at a local and democratic level. Other departments, such as the Home Office, remove the ability of some groups to be part of society, for example asylum seekers, by removing their access to public services and their ability to work, the functionalist identifier of citizenship.

Some government initiatives have an emphasis on promoting social solidarity and capacity building, whilst others focus on social cohesion and the reduction in violence and terrorism, and believe that communities cannot be empowered unless their members feel safe.

Programmes such as the local government White Paper (DCLG, 2006) 'strong and prosperous communities' are encouraging local involvement in decision making and governance. The White Paper (2006) sets out a new agenda giving more power to local authorities and an improved relationship between 'local government and citizens' (DCLG, 2006, p.5). It also identifies that 'Despite the range of new engagement opportunities generated by the proposals, many citizens and community groups will need support to make the fullest use of them' (2006, p.44). This is particularly so in relation to community capacity building, increasing skills and confidence to engage. This again identifies a role for Youth and Community Workers to support this involvement.

The dilemmas posed for Youth and Community Workers as a result of these government initiatives have been discussed throughout this book and are summarized below with suggested strategies for action.

Suggested strategies for action

Work with difference

Chapter 1 set the context of our work and defined active citizenship and community learning. It identified the importance of learning from action, and action as the site of transformation and change. This book adopts a critical/social justice approach in line with the three characteristics of informal education outlined in Chapter 2. This means that we recognize the importance of social divisions (Payne, 2006). The debates within the book have discussed what our role is in relation to these differences. An assimilation approach ignores difference in favour of the dominant cultural norms. I suggest we use an integrationist social justice approach that recognizes and values diversity.

The concept of community has been central to the book, and how it is viewed as both the cause of, and solution to, issues of difference. Communities, and the groups and individuals within them, are not homogenous. Each of them has multiple components and identities. This is one of the factors that Payne (2006) discusses as a reason why communities do not fragment. Each member will have multiple roles, for example as a woman, mother, Pakistani, member of the middle class, which at different times make them part of different groups and communities of interest and place (for example school, work, place of worship). In addition to this Payne argues that there are institutional factors that shape and support the coherence of society and its communities, for example anti-discriminatory legislation.

The discussions within this book have outlined some of the work that is currently being carried out by a range of active citizens and groups to enable the 'empowerment' of community members through their involvement in learning and active involvement processes.

As discussed in Chapter 3 on civic and civil involvement the government's focus on marginalized groups may accentuate difference, in line with Putnam's (2000) notions of bonding social capital, and may threaten rather than produce social cohesion.

For example, work focusing on refugees and migrants may further exclude them by:

1) failing to recognize the other elements of socio-economic and government processes that have caused their exclusion (for example, no recourse to public funds/healthcare, the inability to work);

2) accentuating social bonding within groups rather than bridging between groups, resulting in the stereotyping of groups and resentment of those who do not receive attention.

Make space

Chapter 2, identified three characteristics of informal education, and its role in developing social capital and democratic involvement. The importance of association and work with groups was stressed as a site for critical dialogue that can bring about transformation and change.

Make a cost–benefit analysis

Chapter 3 discussed government policy in relation to civic and civil involvement of community members and started to identify whose benefit it was serving. Putnam's types of capital were used to analyse the outcomes of volunteering and community involvement. The concept of state capital was added to identify outcomes that were primarily for the benefit of statutory bodies at a local and national level. The discussion suggested that part of our informal education role was to analyse critically opportunities and demands being placed on communities and their members. This helps us to make informed decisions about whose value and interest these initiatives serve, and how to prioritize time and resources.

Work with and against the state

The work of the ALAC pilots has been used as an example of community created spaces being supported by government funds and policy. The ALAC pilot programme is an illustration of how Youth and Community Workers, active citizens and their representatives have been able to:

1. influence the development of a curriculum debate;

2. shift the focus from community leaders to active citizens;

3. show evidence of the importance of facilitated group work to enable learning processes;

4. *show the importance of raising critical thinking and practice at a personal, community and global level;*

5. *show the importance of a holistic approach as opposed to divisive work with targeted groups;*

6. *debate how we can work 'in and against the state' to change and influence policy and practice.*

The ALAC programme has been able to utilize and develop effective Youth and Community Work practice, shaped by our principles and approaches, particularly those of Paulo Freire and critical, popular education.

Recognize the complexity of volunteer involvement

Chapter 4 discusses differing types of volunteering and uses a volunteer type framework to identify and analyse the activity taking place. The framework identifies how some volunteers are primarily involved for their own benefit whilst others might be part of movements aiming at social change. Accordingly they will have different degrees of association in groups, and will be doing work 'with' or 'for' communities. It was recognized that volunteers have important local knowledge that may be equally as valuable as a skill in relation to their involvement in the community.

Doing us out of a job?

Chapter 5 makes the case that, despite the plethora of volunteering initiatives and the growth of schemes to support unpaid community leaders, Youth and Community Workers still have an important role as informal educators with all types of volunteers.

Historically, those involved in a voluntary capacity were predominantly engaged in philanthropic activity to moralize, save or control those that they deemed to be a risk or at risk. Others engaged in what would now be termed active citizenship, particularly if they were involved in self help activities within their communities or work places, would most probably have been regarded as political agitators and viewed as a threat. This chapter helps to identify the potential for volunteering to contribute to social capital, and starts to indicate the Youth and Community Worker's role to facilitate this.

Youth and Community Work practice and volunteers are situated alongside historical developments in relation to government initiatives, showing how they continue to influence each other. A survey of community development workers (CDWs) in the UK identified that 'unpaid workers in communities are developing roles previously considered to be the remit of professional workers, this suggests scope for giving greater recognition and support to unpaid CDWs' (Glen and Henderson, 2003, p.1). Rather than 'doing us out of a job' these developments must be viewed as giving Youth and Community Workers an important role to encourage and facilitate such volunteers.

Enable participation at an individual and organizational level

Chapter 6 focused on enabling participation, and looked at barriers to participation at an individual, cultural and social level. I made the case that practice must not focus on individuals in a way that pathologizes them, but that organizational and social change must take place to tackle the factors that prevent people from participation. Woodd, when talking about the development of government social policy, states that there is a 'realization that real empowerment requires a cultural change in institutions and confidence building in individuals' (Woodd, 2007, p.10). Likewise, Creasy, when discussing research with communities in North and East London, identified the requirement for a 'shift in priorities in local and national governance, away from creating pathways to participation through structural reforms to its mechanisms, towards securing institutional cultures which can support community engagement and empowerment' (Creasy, 2007, p.3).

Locate our practice, work towards change

Chapter 7 identifies the importance of inclusive and representative practice and the importance of being proactive at individual, cultural and structural levels. As well as working to informal education principles and practice, this requires awareness of our selves and own perspective, what Freire called developing our cultural identity.

Develop our 'cultural identity'

By 1998 in Teachers as Cultural Workers, Freire moved from simplistic notions of working to empower the oppressed to using the concept of cultural identity, stating 'the importance of the identity of each one of us as an agent, educator or learner, of the educational process is clear, as is the importance of our identity as the product of a tension-filled relationship between what we inherit and what we acquire' (Freire, 1998, p.71). With this perspective he aimed to encourage people to recognize difference expounding what he called 'unity in diversity' (Freire, 1992, p.151). For maximum affect, he argued that oppressed groups should work together.

Work in coalitions

Supporting this approach, Holland et al. (1995) argue that we must acknowledge our own standpoints and 'locate ourselves, and to build coalitions from a recognition of the partial knowledges of our own constructed identities' (1995, p.40). We can then work as allies, as a 'more complex vision of the collective conscientization and struggle against oppression, one which acknowledges difference and conflict and like Freire's vision, rests on the belief in the human capacity to feel, to know and to change' (Holland et al., 1995, p.41).

Companion build

Similarly we must consider how we work with those whose views we may oppose. Ann Curry-Stevens (2004, 2005), in her work on Building Support for Social Justice: Perspectives from an Educator, discusses the pedagogy of and for the privileged. She argues that there is a role for educators engaged in what she calls social justice practice and that there is room to critically educate those who might otherwise be perceived as enemies to transform them into allies. She suggests the 'building of companion commitment to the common good, to build one's civic virtues' (2005, np).

These approaches of coalition and companion building give all workers a role in enabling social justice and transformative action. It does not ignore issues of difference but rather enables people to build campaigns and take action around common goals, with shared principles, even though their individual experience or identity may be different. For example, as a non-disabled person I am able to challenge discriminatory practices against disabled people, and importantly challenge the discriminatory attitudes of other non-disabled people, thereby acting as an ally of disabled people.

Apply informal education principles to community learning

Chapter 8 draws on the earlier chapters to identify how to enable learning environments and uses a framework showing the action learning process from inception to evaluation. It identifies the need to be clearer about what is achieved from learning and for whom.

The contribution of learning in community settings to facilitate spaces for community empowerment is discussed, showing how it has the potential to counter current trends towards individualism. Jeffs and Smith summarized their concerns by stating, 'globalization scatters inherited traditions and constantly corrodes the agencies and structures fostering association and community leaving in its wake insecurity and a fear and distrust of neighbours that sustains individualism' (Jeffs and Smith, 2002, p.61).

To counter these trends, Freire advocated that our work should contribute to social change and 'becomes the "practice of freedom", the means by which men and women deal critically and creatively with reality and discover how to participate in the transformation of the world' (Freire, 1972, p.14).

Chapter 8 also discussed progression and recognition and possible types of accreditation for learning. Youth and Community Work are treated equally as professions applying informal education principles and practice. However, the role of 'expert' professional worker with community activists, to provide training and support, is still not fully recognized in the community work sector. This is evident in 'The Community Development Challenge', reporting on the future for community development, which showed that 'fully rounded training and education, is not widely available . . . and lacks the essential values and depth' (DCLG, 2006, p.33).

Recognize our expertise

Chapter 9 on the requirements for effective practice identifies, as a prerequisite for intervention, that we must first recognize who we are and work from our own professional and personal perspective. This necessitates recognizing that we possess expertise in our role as facilitators of informal education. This is a contentious approach. Writers such as Banks argue for the rejection of a Youth and Community professional (that is an expert working with clients in a clearly defined role) in favour of working as a 'committed practitioner. . . working as an ally with a personal commitment to social change' (1996, p.24). However, I do not believe this is sufficient. In the context of multi-agency working and the increased government emphasis on the development of community leaders it has become essential that we are clear about our role and what we offer.

As stated by Richardson and Wolfe:

> *As practitioners we could remain stuck with a discourse of moral panic, struggling to achieve, or impose the desirable outcome. Alternatively, we could risk responding as learners ourselves and appealing to the learner in others. This second course of action invites us to approach new situations with curiosity and openness, seeking to recognize potential rather than to confirm stereotypes. As we strive to work with people, so we focus upon our and their strengths, rather than upon apparent deficits. (Richardson and Wolfe, 2001, p.xiii)*

We can therefore work as co-educators but with expertise as professional workers enabling those involved in community activity to think critically about the world and enable change and transformation to take place.

Enable education for social change
Importantly working with volunteers and active citizens should be seen as accessible to all. As Mayo states:

> *learning for active citizenship (is not) based upon a deficit model of citizenship education – pouring knowledge into a minority of supposedly inadequate individuals and communities. Professionals and policy-makers, in common with the rest of the population, stand to benefit from Active Learning for Active Citizenship, including learning how to develop strategies to promote social solidarity and social justice, challenging inequalities as well as learning how to listen to those whose voices have been less heard. (Mayo, 2008, p.10)*

Conclusion

This book has shown that there is a continuing role for professional workers, but one which takes into account complexities of the experience of community members, particularly volunteers. For those at the end of the spectrum who act as community activists our role may be that of ally. For those at the other end who are lacking in both experience and association we have an important role to play in relation to facilitating networking, developing skills and knowledge. For all, we have a crucial role in creating space for critical dialogue.

In addition, our relationships with communities and their members means that we are ideally placed to enable them to voice their needs and requirements, and the ways best to meet them, through the process of informal community learning. Our role as professional Youth and Community Workers is particularly important in relation to enabling anti-discriminatory and inclusive practice. This can be done by facilitating participation, reflection and critique regarding the work being undertaken.

We also have an important role as informal educators to contribute to the production of social capital. This is supported by Smith who states that 'Putnam's discussion of social capital provides informal educators with a powerful rationale for their activities' (Smith,

2005, np). Smith cites our long-standing involvement in the generation of associational activities and social networks, the use of dialogue and conversation, and the development of communities through encouraging bridging and social capital. Smith argues that the current social policy which targets intervention with those that are seen as high risk, at risk, or problematic will be counter-productive as this excludes large numbers of active community members. He makes the case for holistic education without targeting by stating, 'youth work, community education and adult education must return to being universal services . . . Targeted work fuels resentment amongst those denied the service, stigmatizes those who receive it, and confirms in the minds of a majority the prejudices they already hold' (Jeffs and Smith, 2002, p.62).

This book has demonstrated that there is a technical and educational role for professional workers in relation to different types of volunteers. The technical support can be delivered regardless of our position in relation to the production of different types of state capital. However, if as critical practitioners we locate ourselves in relation to the state and the third sector, and apply a critical perspective, we will have to make a strategic decision about where we position ourselves and our work in relation to the production of social, human and state capital.

There are therefore three possible approaches that Youth and Community Workers could adopt in relation to social policy initiatives, particularly relating to community empowerment, and cohesion strategies and volunteering. As a result of these initiatives:

1. There may be a reduced or non-existent role for professional Youth and Community Workers as adult education programmes train active citizens to be community leaders, and volunteer programmes provide independent volunteers to meet community and individual (and possibly organizational) needs.

2. Professional Youth and Community Work continues, but primarily with the role of engendering state capital and civic engagement. This would be through supporting government programmes such as the Community in Control White Paper (DCLG, 2008). We can enable 'citizens to engage in shaping services in the public domain, and changing practices and policies in their communities' (Tam, 2005).

3. Professional Youth and Community Workers will work with community members and volunteers, applying the three key characteristics of our work as discussed in Chapter 2. The participants will be facilitated to have association through groups and be involved in critical dialogue. The workers will enable them to act autonomously, and to base their action on voluntary participation and self identified problem posing. They will be facilitated to engage in civil as well as civic engagement, and to support a vibrant civil sector. Finally we will work in a holistic and inclusive way, based on the self identified needs and wishes of communities as opposed to targeted government led intervention.

The dilemma that Youth and Community Workers face is whether we adopt the second approach outlined above and undertake the government agenda at all costs, or whether we strive towards the third option and make sure that the distinctive informal education focus of our work means we take a principled approach and act as facilitators of a truly independent and vibrant civil society. As Smith states:

*the cultivation of the knowledge, skills and virtues necessary for political participation –
is more important morally than any other purpose of public education in a democracy
. . . learning to engage with each other in ways that display mutual respect, a concern
for others' needs and a belief in community. For without this, such democracy as we
have will be subverted, and oppression will flourish. When that happens education
serves the interests of the few. Informal education cannot, therefore be neutral. Our
behaviours and attitudes must convey deep respect for democratic values. We must
build, not destroy democracy.*

(1996, pp.33–34).

One possibility could be that we continue to be committed to making space in which critical
dialogue can take place, within what should be the middle ground of civil society. To enable
this we have to be committed, to be effective professional Youth and Community Workers
who in a time of 'markets, free trade, globalization and the end of ideology . . .' do not '. . .
focus our individual careers on self advancement and exclusion' but more on the 'discourse
of collective work, social justice and equity' (Walker, 1996, p.413). My belief is that we have
a growing role to enable the continuation of an inclusive, vibrant civil society and those
who are active within it.

REFERENCES

Annette, J and Creasy, S (2007) *Individual pathways to participation*. Swindon: ERSC.

Banks, S (1996) Youth work, informal education and professionalization. *Youth and Policy*, 54: 13–25.

Creasy, S (2007) Introduction, in J Annette and S Creasy, *Individual pathways to participation*. Swindon:
ESRC.

Curry-Steven, A (2005) Building support for social justice: Perspectives from an educator, Conference
paper, Canadian Social Welfare Policy Conference, Toronto.

Department of Communities and Local Government (DCLG) (2006) *The community development challenge*.
West Yorkshire: DCLG publications (www.communities.gov.uk).

Department of Communities and Local Government (DCLG) (2006) Local Government White Paper, Strong
and Prosperous Communities. London: DCLG.

Department of Communities and Local Government (2007a) *Local Government and Public Involvement in
Health Act* 2007. London: DCLG.

Department of Communities and Local Government (DCLG) (2007b) *An action plan for community
empowerment: Building on success*. London: DCLG.

Department of Communities and Local Government (DLCG) (2008) *Communities in Control White Paper)*.
London: DCLG.

Department for Children Schools and Families (DfSCF and Treasury) (2007) *Aiming high*. London: DfSC.

Freire, P (1972) *Pedagogy of the oppressed*. London: Penguin Books.

Freire, P (1992) *Pedagogy of hope*. New York: Continuuum

Freire, P (1998) *Teachers as cultural workers: Letters to those who dare teach*. Oxford: Westview Press.

Glen, A. and Henderson, P (2003) *A survey of community development workers in the UK*. London: Community Development Foundation.

Holland, J, Blair, M and Sheldon, S (1995) *Debates and Issues in feminist research and pedagogy*. Milton Keynes: The Open University.

Home Office (HO) (Blunkett, D) (2003) *Active citizens, strong communities – progressing civil renewal*. London: Home Office.

Home Office (HO) (2005) *Communities group strategic plan 2005–6: Helping to build active, cohesive and empowered communities*. London: TSO, Home Office.

Jeffs, T and Smith, M (2002) Individualization and youth work. *Youth and Policy*, I76: 39–65.

Ledwith, M (1997) *Participating in transformation*. Birmingham: Venture Press.

Mayo, M (2008) An overview of active learning for active citizenship, in J Annette and M Mayo, eds, *Active learning for active citizenship*. Nottingham: NIACE.

Payne, G (2006) *Social divisions*. Basingstoke: Palgrave Macmillan.

Prochaska, F (2002) *Schools of citizenship*: *Charity and civic virtue*. London: Civitas.

Putnam, RD (2000) *Bowling alone: The collapse and revival of American community*. New York: Simon and Schuster.

Richardson, LD and Wolfe, M (2001) *Principles and practice of informal education*. London: RoutledgeFalmer.

Smith, MK (2005) *'Robert Putnam'*, *the encyclopaedia of informal education*. London: YMCA, George Williams College (www.infed.org/thinkers/putnam.htm).

Smith, MK (1996) *Local education, community, conversation, praxis*. Buckingham. Open University Press.

Tam, H (2005) *Active citizens*. London: Civil Renewal Unit, Communities Group, Home Office (www. active-citizen.org.uk).

Walker, M (1996) Subaltern professionals: Acting in the pursuit of social justice. *Educational Action Research*, 4 (3): 407–425.

Woodd, C (2007) Active learning for active citizenship: The policy context. *OR Insight*, 20 (2): 8–12.

Glossary

Active citizenship: 'is about being involved in your community, having your say and taking part in decisions that affect you. Above all, it is about people making things happen. This often means taking the opportunity to be actively involved in tackling the things that need to change around you. As a result you will be able to improve the quality of life in your local community. It is not about nationality' (Southwark Volunteer Centre). '[A]ctive citizenship recognizes that the health of communities and society as a whole, is enhanced when people are motivated and able to participate in meeting their needs' through ideas of "mutuality and reciprocity"' (Barr and Hashagen, 2007, p.53).

Active Learning for Active Citizenship (now Take Part): the name given to the (Home Office and then Department of Communities and Local Government in the UK) programme for development of skills and knowledge to enable civil and civic participation by community members. Learning is viewed as an active process which leads to action facilitated by experience and dialogue/conversations and increased personal and community capacity.

Civic: referring to the area of the individuals citizen's relationship to the state, and local and national government, often used in relation to democratic process and includes legal and policy requirements.

Civil: used to refer to the private rights of individuals and the area of relationships between citizens and their organizations.

Civil society: 'refers to the arena of uncoerced collective action around shared interests, purposes and values. In theory, its institutional forms are distinct from those of the state, family and market, though in practice the boundaries between state, civil society, family and market are often complex, blurred and negotiated. Civil society commonly embraces a diversity of spaces, actors and institutional forms, varying in their degree of formality, autonomy and power. Civil societies are often populated by organizations such as registered charities, development non-governmental organizations, community groups, women's organizations, faith-based organizations, professional associations, trade unions, self-help groups, social movements, business associations, coalitions and advocacy groups' (Working definition of the Centre for Civil Society, London School of Economics).

Community: '[A] set of people who have something in common and are connected through interaction and shared interests. This could be based on locality, a shared identity or experience of discrimination' (Gilchrist, 2007, p.viii).

*Conscientization: the process of 'learning to perceive social, political and economic contradictions and to take action against the oppressive elements of reality' (Freire, 1972, p.15). It is about developing consciousness, but consciousness that is understood to have the power to transform reality (Taylor, 1993).

*Dialogue: the process of conversational encounter and exploration with others that enables critical analysis of the world. Dialogue involves respect. It should not involve one person acting on behalf of another, but rather people working with each other.

Empowerment: 'tackling power differentials so as to increase the influence that people can have over the decisions that affect their lives' (Gilchrist, 2007, p.viii).

Engagement: the involvement of community members in processes that primarily produce state capital or are in relation to civic participation, e.g. governance, democratic and government led initiatives.

Human capital: 'physical capital refers to physical objects and human capital refers to properties of individuals' (Putnam, 2000, p.19). Human capital is produced through activity, which is primarily for the benefit of the individual (for example, getting a job as a result of work experience as a volunteer).

Involvement: to take part as a participant, usually in a self directed and community led way, e.g. participating in local community meetings.

Inclusion: in this text it is taken to signify the process of recognizing the rights of individuals and groups, identifying differences and similarities and taking steps to accommodate these. This is not the same as assimilation (where individuals and groups lose their own identity and norms).

Informal education: a (group) process, based on principles of social justice and empowerment, that enables the making of space for facilitated critical dialogue and conscientization of participants who undertake self determination activities leading to transformation, change and improvement. It can take place in any setting, and is influenced by the popular education approach of Paulo Freire.

Participation: being actively involved or sharing in processes and activities that have the potential for action and change: 'participation and active citizenship is about having the right, the means, the space and the opportunity – and where necessary the support – to participate in and influence decisions and engage in action and activities so as to contribute to building a better society (Council of Europe, 2003). Participation and empowerment are integrally linked. Power is fundamental to participation. Participation should increase influence and control, and empowerment cannot take place without participation (Ord, 2007).

*Praxis: a process of reflection and action which embodies certain qualities. These include a commitment to human well being, the search for truth and respect for others. It is informed action and requires that a person 'makes a wise and prudent practical judgement about how to act in *this* situation' (Carr and Kemmis, 1986, p.190). This involves interpretation, understanding and application in 'one unified process' (Gadamer, 1979, p.275).

Problem posing: both worker and participant are in a process of critically exploring reality and so co-creating knowledge. This is problem posing as opposed to problem solving. Problem solving is when individuals or communities are asked or expected by others (e.g. funders, service providers, government agencies) to respond to and remedy situations that other people have identified as problematic, e.g. the behaviour of young people.

Social capital: Putnam (2000) refers to social capital as 'the connections among individuals, social networks and the norms of reciprocity and trustworthiness that arise from them' (2000,

Taken from the Take Part learning framework (www.takepart.org/framework-for-active-learning)

p.19). Social capital is what is produced as a result of activity that is of primary benefit to communities, community groups and their members (for example volunteering to organize a community festival brings benefits of increased neighbourliness, well being and information). See M. Smith, *Social capital* (2007) (http://www.infed.org/biblio/social_capital.htm).

State capital: the benefit that is produced from activity that is primarily for the benefit of the state and statutory authorities and not for community, voluntary or community organizations or individual benefit. This may be evident in relation to financially driven outcomes and targets, geared to meet particular social policy requirements.

REFERENCES

Barr, A and Hashagen, S (2007) *ABCD handbook: A framework for evaluating community development.* London: Community Development Foundation.

Carr, W and Kemmis, S (1986) *Becoming critical: Education, knowledge and action research.* Lewes: Falmer.

Friere, P (1972) *Pedagogy of the oppressed.* London: Penguin.

Gadamer, H-G (1979) *Truth and method.* London: Sheed and Ward.

Gilchrist, A (2007) *Equalities and communities.* London: Community Development Foundation.

Ord, J (2007) *Youth work process, product and practice.* Dorset: Russell House Publishing.

Putnam, RD (2000) *Bowling alone: The collapse and revival of American community.* New York: Simon and Schuster.

Taylor, PV (1993) *The texts of Paolo Freire.* Buckingham: Open University Press.

Tonnies, F (1957) *Community and society: Gemeinschaft und Gesellschaft,* translated and edited by Charles P. Loomis. Ann Arbor: Michigan State University Press.

Index

A

accountability 81, 121, 122–6, 128
accreditation 115–16, 117
achievement recognition 115
action 4–5, 8, 19, 132, 140; community 13, 18; PCS model 99; praxis 64; *see also* collective action
action learning 9, 74–5
active citizenship 4–5, 30, 34, 103, 139; community learning 108–9, 117; definition of 6, 149; diversity 102; education 111, 112; empowerment 90; government promotion of 3, 37–8, 57; inclusive practice 86; outcomes 132; participation 19, 71; reflective practice 135; Russell Commission report 53; types of active citizens 59; volunteering 47–52
Active Learning for Active Citizenship (ALAC) 1, 6–7, 20, 131–2, 141–2, 149; action 8; citizenship dilemmas 98; cognitive dissonance 133; core curriculum 93–4; critical dialogue 15; empowerment 90; Hattersley Neighbourhood Partnership Audit 21; horizontal and vertical involvement 79; migrant workers 74; outcomes 114; self-directed participation 19; SPACE 16; state capital 34; tensions within 39, 108–9; voluntary activity 62; *see also* Takepart
Aiming High 31, 95, 96, 139
ALAC *see* Active Learning for Active Citizenship
Annette, J. 139
anti discriminatory practice 20, 89, 99, 100, 107, 146
antisocial behaviour 2, 96
Arnstein, S.R. 71–2
asylum seekers 35, 36–7, 66, 93, 97, 114, 140
autonomy 31, 110

B

Banks, S. 13, 59, 122, 132, 145
Batsleer, J. 15, 16, 40, 90, 100, 102
Bedford, Jill 117
Berry, H. 88, 93
Black Country Hub 16
Blunkett, David 4–5, 30, 34, 38–9, 108, 117, 138, 139
Brechin, A. 19, 130–1
Building Civil Renewal 30, 31, 32
Butcher, H. 19, 20, 59, 107, 120, 131

C

capital 32–3, 35, 47, 49, 112; *see also* human capital; social capital; state capital
CDWs *see* community development workers
Champions of Participation 71
change 83, 84, 103, 107, 116
Charity Organization Society 57
children 70, 94–5
Citizen Engagement and Public Services: Why Neighbourhoods Matter 30, 31
citizenship: action 4–5; ALAC programme 98; definition of 95; education 112; functionalist approach 95–6; inclusive practice 86, 93–4; outcomes 132; PCS model 97; rights 94–5; voluntary involvement 3–4; young people 95, 96; *see also* active citizenship
Citizenship Review (2008) 3
Citizenship Survey (2005) 49
civic engagement 2, 7, 25, 28–9, 39–40, 71; ALAC programme 108–9; Hattersley Neighbourhood Partnership Audit 21; outcomes 132; state capital 47; volunteering 58; Youth and Community Worker's role 64, 146; *see also* engagement
civil engagement 2, 7, 28–9, 39–40, 71; outcomes 132; volunteering 45; Youth and Community Worker's role 64, 147; *see also* engagement
civil society 16, 28, 32, 71; definition of 149; 'manufactured' 33, 77; 'self-organizing processes' 73; social capital 33, 47; volunteering 35, 44; Youth and Community Worker's role 147
coalitions 100, 143
cognitive dissonance 133
collective action 5, 20, 38, 110; Community Development Challenge 82; empowerment 90; Freirian approaches 14; schools of participation 75
coMMUni project 47, 50, 63
communitarianism 4, 31–2, 39
Communities and Local Government Empowerment White Paper (2008) 37–8, 146
community: definition of 149
community action 13, 18
community activism 48, 49, 51, 145
Community Audit and Evaluation Centre 116
community care 12, 13

community created spaces 77, 78, 79, 80
community development 4, 6, 13, 39; ALAC programme
109; critical approach 120; entry into profession 56;
equality and human rights 87; volunteering 42
Community Development Challenge 81–2, 107, 144
Community Development Foundation 80
community development workers (CDWs) 142
community learning 1, 7–8, 22, 105, 106, 117;
accreditation 115–16; active citizenship 108–9;
informal education 109–11, 144; outcomes and
outputs 114; reflective practice 135; role of the
worker 111–12; template for enabling 112–14;
see also learning
community networks 27, 31, 78
community organization 12, 13, 45
community practice 59
companion building 144
conscientization 14, 20, 90, 92, 100, 107, 127, 143,
149
constructed conversations 73–4
consultation 35
Creasy, S. 139, 143
Crick Report (1998) 94, 97
crime 2, 96
critical consciousness 20, 98, 120, 131
critical dialogue 9, 35, 130, 141; civil society 28; informal
education 8, 14, 15, 107, 127; reflective practice
135–6; volunteering 47; Youth and Community
Worker's role 73, 146–7
critical perspective 19–20, 94, 107, 120, 121, 130–1,
139
critical practice 20, 120, 130–1
critical reflection 20, 63–4, 65, 100, 119, 121, 125,
131
Crow, G. 7–8
cultural identity 143
Curry-Stevens, Ann 144

D
Davies, B. 35
Deaf Linkwork Project 75–6
decision making 3, 6; barriers to participation 87;
community involvement 30, 32; critical
consciousness 120; volunteering 45; women's
under-representation 93, 101
democracy 29, 147; democratic deficit 93; education 94,
111; Freirian approaches 14; informal education 22,
23; participation 71, 77
Department of Communities and Local Government 18,
31, 34, 98, 132

Dewey, John 46, 139
dialogue 13, 14, 20, 63; constructed conversations 73;
definition of 149–50; diverse groups 103; voluntary
activity 62; see also critical dialogue
difference 14, 91–3, 100, 102, 125, 140, 143; see also
diversity
disabled people 62, 109, 144
discrimination 92, 99, 100, 102, 110, 134–5; citizenship
education 94; community development 87; critical
perspective 121, 130; disabled people 144;
empowerment 90; ethical conduct for youth work
125; participation 71; social divisions 91
diversity 8, 86, 91, 94, 102, 140; ALAC programme 98,
103; ethical conduct for youth work 125; Freire 143;
see also difference
domestic abuse 115
double loop learning 128, 130
Dreyfus, H. 45, 47, 49, 51, 60, 61
Dreyfus, S. 45, 47, 49, 51, 60, 61
Dunn, A. 71
'Duty to Involve' 70

E
education 4, 6, 110–11; accreditation 115–16; ALAC
programme 98; citizenship 94, 97, 112; community
7, 12; Freire 14; holistic 146; reflective practice
120–1; Refugee Charter 36; social change 145;
social justice 144; see also informal education;
learning
effective practice 119–35, 145; accountability 122–6;
community learning 135; strategy options 133–5;
taking action 132; training 120–1
employers, accountability to 123
employment: migrant workers 74; Refugee Charter 36
empowerment 2, 7, 20, 53, 80, 90, 139; ALAC
programme 6, 98; Building Civil Renewal 31;
citizenship 94; community development 87;
definition of 150; Freirian approaches 14;
government initiatives 140; participation 70,
71, 84, 143; participatory democracy 29;
'sustainable communities' 42; volunteering 66;
young people 96
engagement 2, 5, 22, 26; definition of 150; government
emphasis on 30, 57, 140; participation 70;
self-directed 18; volunteering 47; see also civic
engagement; civil engagement; involvement;
participation
equality 86, 87, 90, 98, 100–2, 110
ethical conduct 122, 124–5
ethical dilemmas 132, 133, 134

ethnic minorities 62, 87, 94
Etzioni, Amitai 31, 44
Every Child Matters 70, 95
evidence based practice 131
expertise 46, 50, 51, 52, 60, 63, 67, 145

F
feminism 95, 120
Festinger, L. 133
festivals 27
Field, J. 32–3, 38, 53
Forrester, K. 111
Freire, Paulo 9, 13–14, 20, 86, 106, 111; conscientization
    90, 92; cultural identity 143; praxis 119; reflection
    63, 64; social change 144
Freirian approaches 1, 14, 18, 20, 37; ALAC programme
    98, 109; community learning 112; schools of
    participation 75
Friends of Al Buraq 27
Friends of Manley Park 26, 27
functionalist approach 95–6, 140
funding 77, 80–1, 131
Future Builders 30

G
Gardner, P. 98
Garratt, D. 2–3
GEM (Gender and Community Engagement in
    Manchester) project 87–8, 93, 101
gender mainstreaming 101
Gilchrist, Alison 81, 86–7, 90, 101, 106
Goldsmith, Lord QC 3
Gorbing, Sue 117
government initiatives 3, 25, 26, 27, 30; active
    citizenship 49; participation 76–7; social capital 32,
    33, 37–8; state capital 33–5, 140; volunteering 43,
    48, 57, 71; see also state
Gramsci, A. 111
Groundwork 116
groups 15, 16, 72–4, 97; informal education 107;
    learning 107–8, 110, 113–14, 117

H
Hattersley Neighbourhood Partnership Audit 21, 23, 83
healthcare: asylum seekers 114; migrant workers 74;
    participation 78; Refugee Charter 36
Healthy Living Network (HLN) 20, 116
Hodgson, L. 33, 38, 48, 77
Holland, J. 143
housing: migrant workers 74; Refugee Charter 36

human capital 32, 38, 39, 40, 46, 67; ALAC programme
    109; definition of 150; informal education 23, 110;
    positive and negative consequences 35;
    volunteering 47–8, 49, 50–2, 53, 58
human rights 14, 87, 100, 110

I
identity 94, 107, 143
Impact! Programme 16–17, 23
inclusion 6, 69, 86–104; barriers to 87; citizenship 93–4;
    commitment to 20; critical consciousness 120;
    definition of 150; informal education 107; see also
    diversity
individual action 5
inequality 20, 71, 87, 92, 97, 103, 134–5
informal education 9, 12–24, 97, 106–7, 141, 147;
    action 8; ALAC programme 98; citizenship 94;
    community learning 109–11, 117, 144; curriculum
    framework 39; definition of 150; participation 71–2,
    79, 80, 81; PCS model 99; potential for change 116;
    reflective practice 127–8, 135–6; volunteering 56,
    61–4
involvement 2, 3–4, 25–41; ALAC 6; barriers to 65;
    definition of 150; Freire 14; horizontal and vertical
    79; self-directed 18–19; volunteering 54, 59; see
    also engagement; participation

J
Jeffs, T. 12, 13, 14, 22, 23, 144
Jensen, M.A.C. 72
Job Centres 76
Jochum, V. 38

K
Knott, C. 127
knowledge: co-production of 130, 135, 150; volunteers
    46, 47, 60, 61, 63, 64, 120
Kolb, D. 89

L
La Verneda project 61
ladder of participation 71–2
language issues 65
learning 7–8, 62, 89, 105–18; accreditation 115–16,
    117; active 8, 63, 103, 108, 149; co-production of
    knowledge 130; experiential 6, 52, 139; group 73,
    107–8, 117; informal education 106–7, 109–11,
    144; outcomes and outputs 114, 132; reflective
    practice 126, 128; role of the worker 111–12; safe
    space for 17; schools of participation 74–5; social

theory of 15, 107; template for enabling 112–14; *see also* Active Learning for Active Citizenship; community learning
Ledwith, Margaret 13, 20, 69, 107, 120, 139
legal requirements 123, 128, 129
liberal approach 94–5
local authority initiatives 25, 26, 27, 35
local government 71, 77, 139, 140
Local Government and Public Involvement in Health Act (2007) 32, 70
Local Network Fund 49

M
Maclean, C. 7–8
management accountability 126
Manchester Metropolitan University: coMMUni project 47, 50, 63; Community Audit and Evaluation Centre 116
Manchester Refugee and Migrant Forum 97
Manchester Refugee Charter 36–7
manufactured spaces 77, 78, 79, 80
Marshall, T.H. 95, 97
Mayo, M. 6, 23, 110–11, 145
migrant workers 74

N
National Council for Voluntary Organizations 16, 31, 38
national identity 94
National Youth Work Agency 89
Neighbours Days 49
New Labour 4, 7, 26, 39, 44, 57, 87, 138

O
Occupational Standards for Community Development 81–2, 109
Ord, J. 18
Oteyza, C. 88, 93

P
participation 69–85, 86; active citizenship 71; ALAC programme 19, 98; atmosphere factors 83; barriers to 62, 69, 82, 83, 84, 87–8, 102; community development 87; definition of 150; democratic citizenship 110; effectiveness of workers 80–2; enabling 72, 79, 82, 102, 143; importance of 69, 80; individual factors 83; informal education 71–2, 94, 107; ladder of 71–2; schools of 20, 74–6; social policy 70; social theory of learning 108; spaces for 77–80; task factors 83; types of groups 72–4; volunteering 53, 61–2; *see also* engagement; involvement

participatory budgeting 77
Payne, M. 15, 92, 97, 140
PCS model 88–9, 97, 99, 114, 121
philanthropy 43, 44, 53
physical capital 32, 47
Piper, H. 2–3, 8
policing 27, 78
policy 2–3, 4, 16, 29–31, 139; community learning 108; difference 91–3; participation 70; state capital 35; targeting 146; volunteering 58, 66
Popple, K. 12–13, 28, 49
poverty 71, 83, 87, 110
power 3, 13, 20, 64, 86, 101; active citizenship 5, 6; civil and civic spheres 29; critical perspective 121; Deaf Linkwork Project 75–6; social order 90
praxis 9, 14, 20, 119, 120, 127; co-learning 64; definition of 150; informal education 107; voluntary activity 62
private sector 28, 44, 58
problem posing 14, 18–19, 75, 107, 127, 150
problem solving 18, 127, 150
Prochaska, F. 43, 44, 139
public sector 28
Putnam, R.D.: diversity 8, 102; 'doing for/doing with' distinction 46, 51, 52, 111; social capital 30, 34, 46, 76, 141, 146; types of capital 9, 32, 33, 47–8; volunteering 44, 53

Q
qualifications 115–16

R
RARPA (Recognizing and Recording Progress and Achievement) 115
reflection 9, 14, 119, 126–8; ALAC programme 98; community learning 135; praxis 150; volunteers 63, 64; *see also* critical reflection
reflective practice 20, 92, 119, 120–1, 126–31, 135–6; accountability 126; case studies 129; community learning 112, 135; critical perspective 130–1; taking action 132
Refugee Charter 36–7
representative practice 92–3
responsibilities 95
Richardson, L.D. 145
rights 14, 20, 94–5; ALAC programme 98; migrant workers 74; Refugee Charter 36; *see also* human rights
Robertson, J. 59
Russell Commission on Youth Action and Engagement 43, 45, 53, 62

S

Scarman Trust 49
Schön, Donald 119, 126, 128, 131, 133
schools of participation 20, 74–6
Scragg, T. 127
self accountability 125
self determination 42, 86, 98, 107, 120
self help 18, 20, 39, 142; capital 48; empowerment 90;
    enabling 62; volunteering 45, 49, 57, 66
'self-organizing processes' 73
service users 123, 129
Shaull, R. 14
single loop learning 128
Single Regeneration Budget 33
skills 45, 60, 61, 63, 64
Smith, M. 12, 13, 14, 22, 23, 144, 146, 147
social capital 4, 8, 30, 32–3, 37–8, 40; active citizenship
    37, 90; bridging 32–3, 93, 97, 102; building 103;
    community learning 112; definition of 150–1;
    'doing for/doing with' distinction 46; education 110;
    group work 16; Hattersley Neighbourhood
    Partnership Audit 21; horizontal community
    engagement 76; informal education 23; negative
    consequences 34, 35, 141; positive consequences
    35; representative practice 93; volunteering 47–8,
    49, 50–2, 53, 58, 62, 67; Youth and Community
    Worker's role 146
social cohesion 2, 36, 102, 138, 140, 141
social control 57, 58, 96
social divisions 88–9, 91, 92, 103, 140
social exclusion 3, 32, 62, 74, 92, 110, 138
social justice 8, 86, 89, 100, 110; ALAC programme
    6, 7, 98; commitment to 9, 20; community
    development 87; companion building 144; critical
    consciousness 120; critical practice 130; diversity
    140; ethical conduct for youth work 125; informal
    education 107, 128; promotion of 145;
    representative practice 92
social order 31, 90
social policy 2–3, 4, 16, 29–31, 139; community
    learning 108; participation 70; state capital 35;
    targeting 146
social work 89
solidarity 4, 5, 6, 102, 120, 140, 145
space 15–16
state 29, 33, 139, 141–2; public sector 28; volunteering
    44, 56, 58, 67; Youth and Community Worker's role
    67, 146; see also government initiatives
state capital 9, 33–5, 38, 40, 139, 140; definition of 151;
    Hattersley Neighbourhood Partnership Audit 21;

informal education 23; positive and negative
    consequences 35; volunteering 47, 48, 49, 50, 52,
    53; Youth and Community Worker's role 64, 146
stereotypes 91, 99
Storrie, T. 49
strategic regeneration frameworks 27, 78
Strong and Prosperous Communities 32, 57, 140
Sure Start 33, 81
'sustainable communities' 42, 82

T

Takepart 5, 62, 102–3; learning framework 7, 8, 19, 22,
    66, 114; website 10; see also Active Learning for
    Active Citizenship
targeted policy 146
third sector 28, 29–30, 33, 37, 39, 44–5, 58, 146; see
    also volunteering
Thomas, D.N. 67
Thompson, N.: diversity 91; empowerment 90, 92; PCS
    model 88–9, 97, 121; reflective practice 126, 127,
    131; worker's role 100
Together We Can 30, 34, 123
training 120–1, 144; see also education
transformation 14, 20, 23, 107, 111, 116
Tuckman, B.W. 72
Twelvetrees, A. 106

V

V programme 30
vertical participation 76, 79
voice 15, 70
voluntary assistance 48–9
volunteering 2–3, 9, 42–55, 138, 139, 142; ALAC 6;
    barriers to 64, 65; categories of volunteer 45–7,
    120; civil society 35; Communities and Local
    Government Empowerment White Paper 37–8;
    Community Audit and Evaluation Centre courses
    116; composition of volunteers 53; definition of 43;
    government intervention 39, 44–5, 58, 71; informal
    education 61–4; participatory evaluation 50–2;
    support requirements 60–1; types of 42–3, 59–60;
    V programme 30; Why Neighbourhoods Matter 31;
    young people 96; Youth and Community Worker's
    role 54, 56–68, 146; see also third sector

W

Walker, M. 63, 147
Walzer, M. 28
ward coordination 27, 78, 80
Wenger, E. 15, 107–8

Why Neighbourhoods Matter 30, 31
Wolfe, M. 145
women 99, 100; ALAC programme 109; domestic
abuse 115; feminist framework 120; GEM
project 87–8, 93, 101; Impact! Programme
16–17; under-representation in decision making
93, 101
Woodd, Charles 59–60, 143
Woodward, V. 90, 98, 101, 103, 108

Y

Year of the Volunteer 48
Young, Kerry 14, 120
young offenders 35, 88

young people: advice and guidance to 88; Aiming High
31, 95, 96, 139; citizenship 95, 96; diversity 102;
ethical conduct for youth work 124–5; National
Youth Work Agency 89; right to participation 70;
volunteering 46, 53, 62; youth opportunities
funding 76–7
Youth and Community Workers 1, 4, 5, 138, 142, 145–7;
accountability 122–6; civil and civic engagement
40; community learning 8, 111–12, 113, 114;
context of work 56–60; effectiveness 80–2; group
facilitation 73; informal education 12–24, 106;
ladder of participation 72; models for practice
98–100; volunteering 38, 54, 56–68
Youth Matters 30, 53, 62